# Global Research Without Leaving Your Desk

## CHANDOS
### INFORMATION PROFESSIONAL SERIES

Series Editor: Ruth Rikowski
(e-mail: Rikowskigr@aol.com)

Chandos' new series of books are aimed at the busy information professional. They have been specially commissioned to provide the reader with an authoritative view of current thinking. They are designed to provide easy-to-read and (most importantly) practical coverage of topics that are of interest to librarians and other information professionals. If you would like a full listing of current and forthcoming titles, please visit our website www.chandospublishing.com or e-mail info@chandospublishing.com or telephone +44 (0) 1223 891358.

**New authors:** we are always pleased to receive ideas for new titles; if you would like to write a book for Chandos, please contact Dr Glyn Jones on e-mail gjones@chandospublishing.com or telephone number +44 (0) 1993 848726.

**Bulk orders:** some organisations buy a number of copies of our books. If you are interested in doing this, we would be pleased to discuss a discount. Please e-mail info@chandospublishing.com or telephone +44(0) 1223 891358.

# Global Research Without Leaving Your Desk: Travelling the world with your mouse as companion

JANE MACOUSTRA

Chandos Publishing

*Oxford • Cambridge • New Delhi*

Chandos Publishing
TBAC Business Centre
Avenue 4
Station Lane
Witney
Oxford OX28 4BN
UK
Tel: +44 (0) 1993 848726
E-mail: info@chandospublishing.com
www.chandospublishing.com

Chandos Publishing is an imprint of Woodhead Publishing Limited

Woodhead Publishing Limited
Abington Hall
Granta Park
Great Abington
Cambridge CB21 6AH
UK
www.woodheadpublishing.com

First published in 2010

ISBN:
978 1 84334 366 0

British Library Cataloguing-in-Publication Data.
A catalogue record for this book is available from the British Library.

Typeset by Domex e-Data Pvt. Ltd.
Printed in the UK and USA.

Printed in the UK by 4edge Limited - www.4edge.co.uk

This book is dedicated to my wonderful sons
James and Samuel

# Disclaimer

Every care has gone into the preparation of this work, which has been double-checked for accuracy before publication. However, the author and publisher cannot be held liable for any inaccuracies that arise through sources and web pages evolving or being removed on the internet. The internet changes every day, so we hope that you will be appreciative of the difficulties faced in keeping this work completely up to date. If you want to keep up with any further alterations that we find in the contents of this book consult *http://www.globalresearcher.wordpress.com*.

# Contents

# List of figures

## Figures

# About the author

Jane has been an information professional for 29 years and is very passionate about her work. It has taken her around the world and she has been able to enjoy the diversity of working with people from many different countries, enhancing her understanding of the information profession and its related disciplines crossing boundaries and cultures. Her experiences are varied and include research, mentoring, teaching and records management. Some of this work was undertaken in Asia, where precious documentation is at risk from humidity, pests and storm damage, which is not experienced in more temperate parts of the world.

Jane has been privileged to have worked with some of the best lawyers in the investment banking industry. Her experiences have enabled her to form professional bonds with colleagues globally and she maintains contact with her peers wherever they are located.

Jane's professional experiences include working for a very large British oil and gas company, a prestigious investment bank in England and Hong Kong, a magic circle law firm in Hong Kong, another eminent City law firm in London, project managing in a large county council and teaching information literacy at a London university. In addition to this she provides private client work trading as Tai-Pan Research, which is her small consultancy business.

Jane's skills include teaching, researching, writing and creating databases, negotiating contracts, managing records, current awareness, controlling large budgets, law, compliance and planning for new libraries to be built. This book is her latest venture, encompassing some of the exciting and interesting things she has learned on her journey, with her mouse as companion.

Jane's next project is an Open University Masters in counselling for battered spouses, a very important topic for her.

Jane has played an active part in her industry, and joined the Special Libraries Association in 2000. In 2007 Jane was awarded the Special Libraries Association Presidential Citation Award for her work as President of the SLA Asian Chapter from 2004 to 2006. She serves on the boards of SLA Europe and SLA Asia as Director.

Jane has worked as a masterclass teacher and speaks at conferences. She has had the privilege of working with one of her heroines on two occasions at Internet Librarian International – MaryDee Ojala.

Jane has been a frequent contributor to the Freepint website on the Bar and Student Bar to assist with hard research questions. Some of the questions have included assisting students with the Sarbanes-Oxley Act 2002, which is an extraordinarily difficult piece of US legislation.

If you like Jane's book, tell her. If you don't like it then tell her as well and tell her why. Constructive criticism is good for everyone to enable them to improve their skills. If you would like copies of Jane's masterclasses or presentations, she will send them to you on application.

Jane can be contacted at taipan.research@gmail.com or you can leave a comment at *http://www.globalresearcher.wordpress.com*, where she can respond to you.

# Acknowledgements

We acknowledge the work contributed by Cameron Bradley from Overton Grange, Sutton, Surrey, who gave us his time on this project in order to hone his internet research skills as part of his work experience in May 2007. At the time, Cameron was a 15-year-old student who enjoyed studying design technology, maths and PE.

Thanks and acknowledgements also to Alan Davenport, Brian Murphy, Garry Elliott and members of Sutton Tennis and Squash Club, current top UK tennis club.

# Preface

The internet is a very fast-moving medium and can be an inexhaustible tool for research. Learning how to put it to effective use takes time, which the reader may not necessarily have. There is much information emerging in relation to new developments and new tools, which are appearing at such a prolific pace that it can take a huge effort to keep up with them. This books aims to give readers a quick reference guide to how the internet and its many components can assist serious researchers to locate business information and reliable sources quickly, while being able to ignore the unreliable information that can be posted. All you need is your computer and your mouse to take an interesting and insightful global tour. Fly around the globe in the fast lane or take the slow boat to China and savour the diversity of information that is available.

Business research takes many different forms; topics range from the social sciences to industry, companies, finance, investment and law, and it is a huge area to research. We are going to attempt to address as many areas as possible within the remit of this book. We are assuming that readers have already attained a certain level of internet skills and will not require being taught the basics of how to use search engines.

The resources we will be looking at are mainly global, but we will also address subjects by country as necessary, highlighting the best resources available for quick access to different types of content. We will also look at major business issues of topical interest such as terrorism, how to know your customer and corruption, and take a look at the 'dark web', which is an emerging concept for those who do not work in the defence industry.

Also of interest to many is Web 2.0, the next generation of social networking tools, which has evolved very quickly. It has captured the attention of information professionals in the workplace, who are implementing these concepts in their libraries and information centres, and it is also being embraced by the general public. The use of wikis, blogs, RSS feeds, Instant Messenger (IM), Voice over Internet Protocol

(VoIP), podcasts, webcasts, virtual worlds and other technologies is now commonplace for the advertising of information services directly to the target audience in large corporations and smaller public library entities. In some of these environments Web 2.0 has been embraced with gusto. Whether it is an over-rated phenomenon is another matter. However, these days there's no need to jump on an aeroplane for long haul journeys, when the technology is available to interact with colleagues across the world in any time zone. The younger generation has taken to these technologies as another way to maintain contact with friends who live afar. Many schools have started to embrace the way these technologies can be used to their advantage, but there's further to go – maybe this book will inspire teachers in schools and institutions of higher education to exploit the possibilities even more. The future lies with the next generation of users and teachers discovering (free) ways to interact with home-educated pupils, or those who may be unable to attend school because of illness, but can still learn from their home environment. Physical location is now secondary to learning and communication.

We hope you enjoy your travels with your mouse to keep you company.

# Tools and search engines, and their characteristics

## Tools

Search engines are not always the best places to locate good information: 'Instead of fighting the Google and Yahoo wars, B2B firms should find better results by searching for and submitting sites to vertical search engines and directories.'[1]

### Get started

Serious researchers have at least three tabs open to enable them to navigate without losing the initial trail of their search. This is because when you conduct research, your lateral thought processes can take you off on tangents that you maybe hadn't initially even thought about. We won't be looking at Boolean operators, as we expect that you already know about them. If you don't, look at Pandia (*http://www.pandia.com/goalgetter/4.html*), which provides a simple and accurate description of the Boolean logic concept. Many search engines already incorporate Boolean logic into their search engine strategies, so you don't normally have to worry about using it.

Always think about acronyms, antonyms and synonyms when structuring your search criteria. Are you using British or American spelling?

There are so many search engines and other tools that it can get confusing. An article by Wendy Boswell who works at About will guide you through the maze of search engines that you can access (Figure 1.1).[2]

**Figure 1.1** '100 Search Engines in 100 Days' on About.com

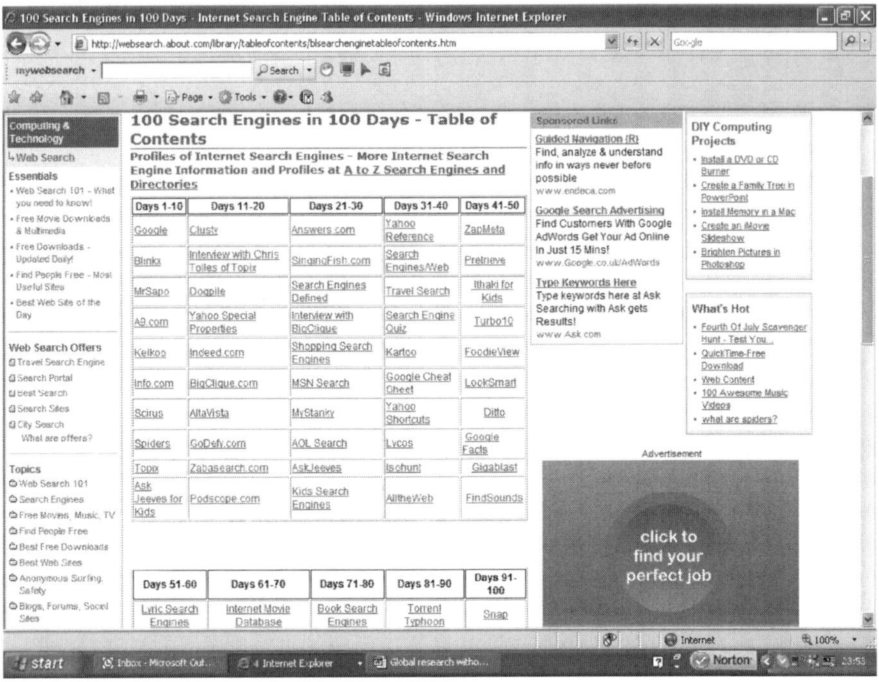

## Read the URL and smarten up your research

Many people don't bother to read the URL before they open a hyperlink. This is a waste of precious research time. If you don't know how to read a URL, you would need to open every hyperlink that you think might be of value to your work. Many people don't bother to do this before they open a web page; they just click through anything that looks relevant. But URLs can tell you a lot about the site content; you would not open many of the pages you come across if you could recognise inappropriate content for your research in the first instance.

There's a useful tutorial from Berkeley University on how to read a URL at *http://www.lib.berkeley.edu/TeachingLib/Guides/Internet/Evaluate .html* (Figure 1.2).[3]

**Tip:** Did you check when this web page was last updated before you decided to read or use it? Is it still relevant?

Right-click on your mouse on the web page to view the source of the page, which can point you to additional keywords and information about what you are looking at.

**Figure 1.2** Tutorial on the Berkeley University website on how to read a URL

# Work out your travelling plan

Depending on the research, good old pen and paper can assist you to make a mind map as you go.

## OneLook: *http://www.onelook.com*

If you are uncertain of your subject, a good resource is the OneLook Dictionary, which also has a reverse look-up facility (see Figures 1.3 and 1.4). I have noticed recently that outsiders can now amend the content of OneLook, so caution may be required when using some of it. It's looking a bit more like a wiki than when it was in its original form, and I was disappointed to see the professional, clean image undermined by smileys and adverts, which detract from the original good product.

Make a note of what you have looked up and verify the terminology if you are in doubt about its authenticity. Use the OU dictionary, Merriam-Webster links or another reputable dictionary to ascertain you have the correct terminology for the research. By adding extra keywords to your search, you can enhance the research outcome.

**Figure 1.3**  OneLook dictionary search page

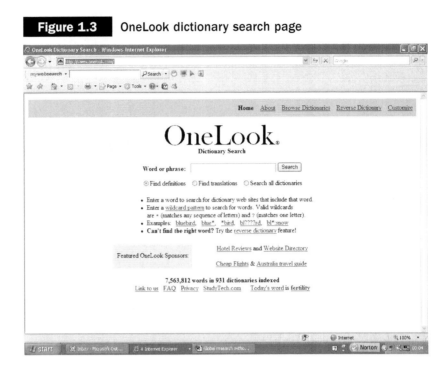

**Figure 1.4**  OneLook showing words and phrases matching a search term

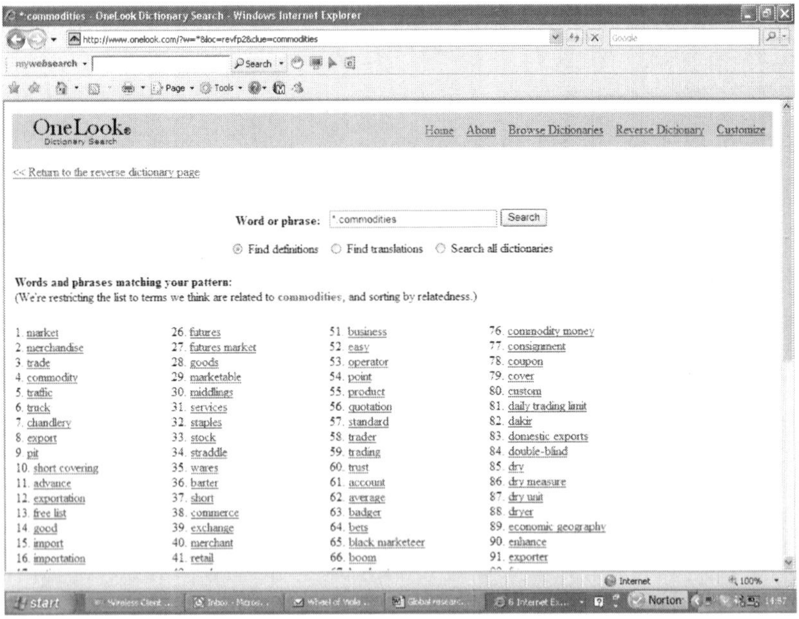

A mind map can take many forms. There's no right or wrong way to create one. Everyone's mind works in different ways. Here are keywords that could form a mind map:

Commodities
Futures
Delivery
Trading
Exchanges
Coupons OR Certificates
Arbitrage
Short selling
Put options
Call options

The keywords were found by looking for one word: Commodities. The commodity was unspecified. Then you could select the most relevant keywords to enhance the search criteria. Now take it into the context of the commodity market:

COMMODITIES
futures market
a commodity exchange where futures contracts are traded

FUTURES CONTRACTS
bulk commodities bought or sold at an agreed price for delivery at a specified future date

TRADING
buying or selling securities or commodities

COMMODITIES EXCHANGE
an exchange for buying and selling commodities for future delivery

COMMODITY MONEY
money for purchasing the commodity

COUPON
a negotiable certificate that can be detached and redeemed as needed

DRY MEASURE
a unit of capacity for dry commodities (such as fruit or grain)

ARBITRAGE
a kind of hedged investment that is meant to capture slight differences in price; when there is a difference in the price of something on two different markets the arbitrageur simultaneously buys at the lower price and sells at the higher price

FUNGIBLE
a commodity that is freely interchangeable with another in satisfying an obligation

SHORT SALE
the purchase of securities or commodities by a short seller to close out a short sale

STRADDLE
the option to buy or sell a given stock (or stock index or commodity future) at a given price before a given date; consists of an equal number of put and call options.

Tip: Look up oil markets and commodities, and some of the same keywords will appear as relevant to this subject, because oil is a commodity. You will also be able to narrow down the search by oil type, such as Brent Crude, and also by where the commodity is traded. You

**Figure 1.5**   ICE home page

would also get pointers to look at OPEC and the Intercontinental Exchange (ICE; *https://www.theice.com/homepage.jhtml*). See Figure 1.5.

Firefox has a tagging add-on called Search Cloudlet (*http://www .getcloudlet.com/*), which has the same function as making a mind map yourself, but it is created via Google or Yahoo! search engines. The tag clouds will show related topics on the screen, giving pointers to other areas for research. See Figure 1.6.

**Figure 1.6**   Result of search on Google for 'derivatives'

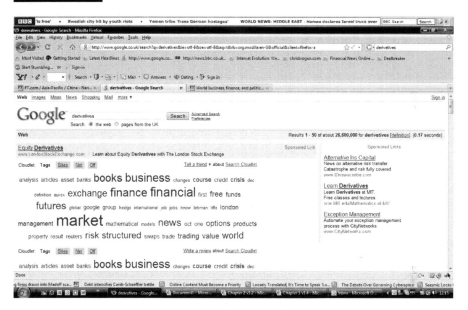

# Track down URLs that don't exist any more

### The Internet Archive: *http://www.archive.org/index.php*

The Internet Archive is useful if you book-marked a uniform resource locator (URL) but the page doesn't exist any more.

'Around the World in 2 billion pages'

The Internet Archive doesn't just archive old web pages and sites; it archives music, moving images, audio software, education and much more. It also has its own blog.

The internet moves daily, with old pages or websites being removed and new ones being added. It is a continuous mass of movement that is virtually impossible to keep up with. What is current one day is obsolete the next, which can be very frustrating for the researcher. You'll tell yourself 'but I knew it was there because I saw it recently'. You really need to locate a certain page or website that you had previously book marked. How do you get it back?

You can either try and view the cached page of the original hyperlink via a search engine such as Google, which will give you a snapshot of the original data that was indexed by the spider, or you can use the Wayback Machine and see if it was indexed there by the spiders before the page/website was removed.

The Internet Archive is a very useful tool to have at your disposal for just this problem. There's no guarantee it will be there, but the Internet Archive is a growing medium for this specific problem.

Here is an example. Drop the URL into the Wayback Machine (*http://web.archive.org/collections/web.htm*) and click on 'Take Me Back'. See Figure 1.7.

The Wayback Machine has indexed more than 85 billion pages and is continuously growing. Between 2004 and 2006, the Wayback Machine

**Figure 1.7** Wayback Machine on Internet Archive

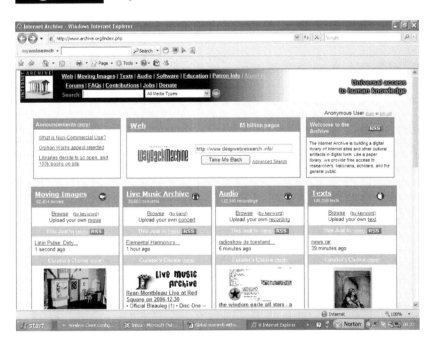

indexed the web page in the diagram that I wanted many times. Now all that is required is to select which date is needed to view the page or website. The asterisk against a date shows when the page was last updated. See Figure 1.8.

**Figure 1.8**   Search results on the Wayback Machine on Internet Archive

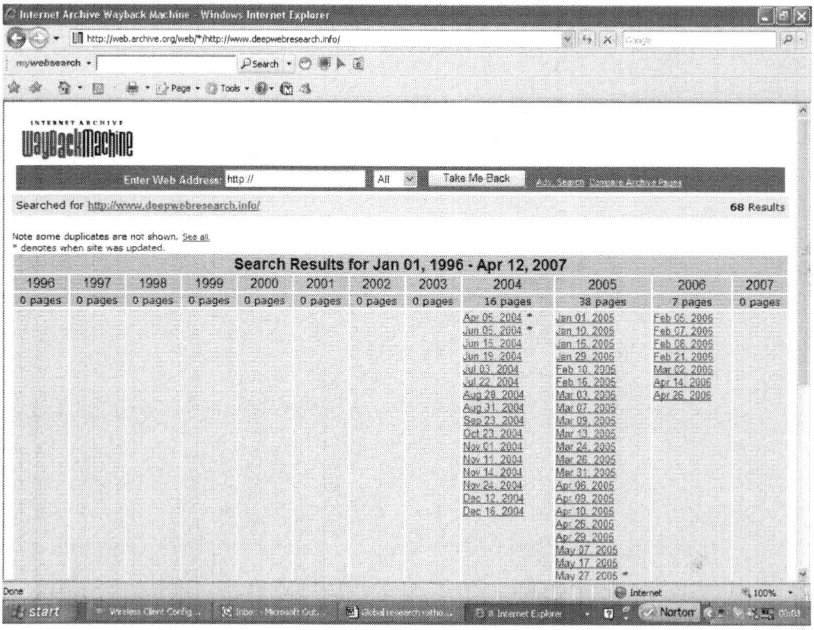

# Search engines and their characteristics

Let's start our journey by flying to Athens and taking a cruise aboard one of the new ferries in the Aegan Sea, around a few search engines. There are so many to choose from that it can get confusing so we will drop anchor at a few ports. We can make an analogy that we are going island-hopping. We may have visited the bigger Greek islands before, but there are some smaller ones that may be still unexplored.

## Google: http://www.google.com/

Everyone uses it, but how they use it differs immensely. We are not going to go into detail about using Google, because most people use it as their default destination when they use the internet. Many people still believe that Google has the answer to all their questions. Well, that's not

**Figure 1.9** Google's Cheat Sheet

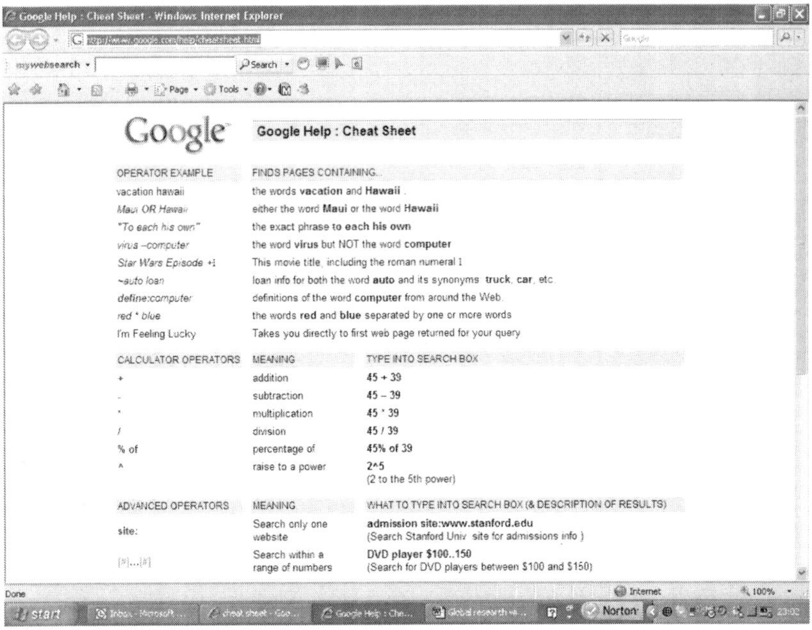

necessarily so. The way that Google is used by many people leaves a lot to be desired. One of the best ways to use Google is to learn about the Cheat Sheet (*http://www.google.com/help/cheatsheet.html*). See Figure 1.9.

By using the advanced operators within the cheat sheet, you will be able to locate the information required a lot faster, and leave the undesirable information where it should be (ignored). Who wants thousands of results when you can compact your query down to the few most relevant results?

Also, always go past the first 10 hits to locate relevant results, and adjust the results to view either the first 50 or 100 results. The results are ranked using complex mathematical algorithms. You can read about these algothithms on the Google website at *http://www.google.com/corporate/tech.html*. You can find relevant results further down the list because of the way that Google indexes it pages. For more information on Google's indexing see the Google Librarian article describing page rank algorithms.[4]

Google Librarian (*http://librariancentral.blogspot.com/*) is a great resource for the education community, librarians and information professionals. Among other resources, it contains free posters that you can print, copyright free, which makes a change in this copyright obsessed world. The articles are written by well-respected information professionals in our field of expertise.

**Figure 1.10** Google Chrome

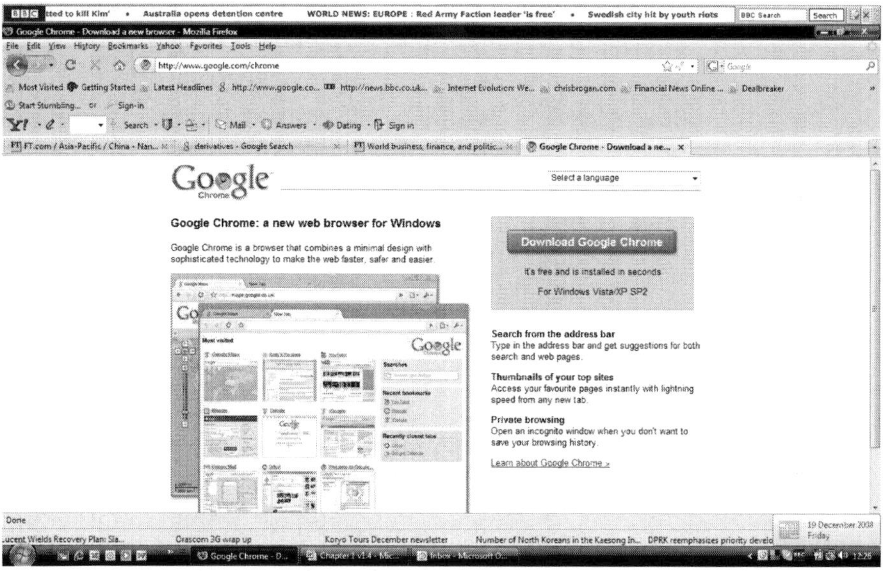

Google Chrome (*http://www.google.com/chrome*) is the latest browser Google has launched and it is easy to use. See Figure 1.10.

The interface displays the most recent searches made and saves your complete browsing history. You can delete these records at any time. It will also allow you to run 'incognito' searches.

## Clusty: *http://clusty.com/*

Clusty has a hierarchical clustering mechanism, and will give you pointers to topics related to the one that you have searched for, clustered by subject. See Figure 1.11.

The clustering mechanism is shown on the left-hand side of the screen. At the bottom of the first set of clusters is the option 'more'. Click on it for more clusters and keywords by subject. Click on a specific subject within the clustered list to delve deeper into a relevant subject. Be aware that the un-numbered results at the top can be paid-for sponsored links and not necessarily relevant to your search, as the sponsors may want to sell you something when you look for information. In the search shown, this is not the case.

Clusty also has an advance search facility. A very general search for banking laws in Asia will bring clustered results by country, so you can narrow down the search to a specific jurisdiction.

**Figure 1.11**  Result of search on Clusty for 'banking laws asia'

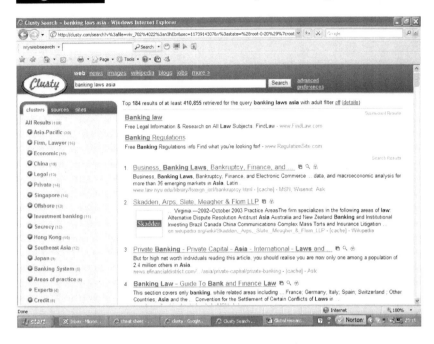

## Turbo 10: *http://turbo10.com/searchthedeepnet.html*

Turbo 10 has some overlap with the search engines, but I have found relevant information through Turbo 10 that I haven't managed to locate elsewhere, which is why I still use it. It calls itself a deep net tool, but it has more of a metasearch functionality about it and it covers results that search engines cannot locate. See Figure 1.12.

At the time of writing, there were over 800 deep net engines to select from. Turbo 10 is intuitive, so it is not necessary to give detailed explanations. One of the newer aspects of Turbo 10 is that it now has a visual aid that shows the home page of the results it locates, which is similar to Exalead. There are other search and metasearch tools that have a visual aid to searching, but in my experience the results have been variable.

Add your customised list on particular subjects of engines that you want to use regularly to the Turbo 10 collections box and save them for future use. It loads quickly and provides a clean layout, but only displays four results per page. When you analyse tools such as these, always use the same search criteria so you can make a comparable assessment of the results with the other tools.

**Figure 1.12**   Turbo 10 search screen

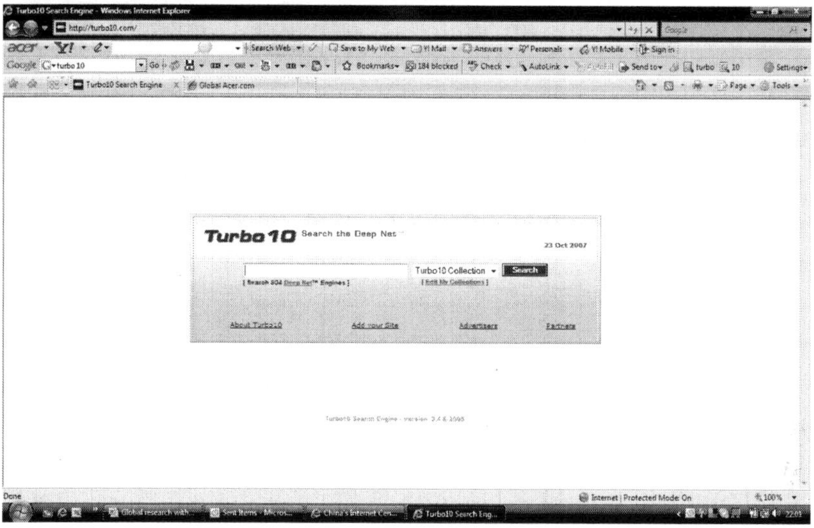

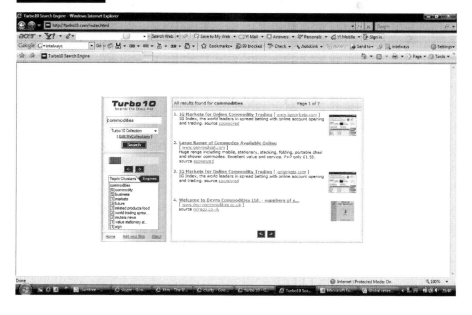

Compare what engines are searched when it is given random choice. In the search shown in Figure 1.13, I allowed Turbo 10 to select its own engines when searching for 'commodities'.

**Figure 1.13**   Result of search on Turbo 10 for 'commodities'

## Figure 1.14 Turbo 10 facility 'Add My Collection'

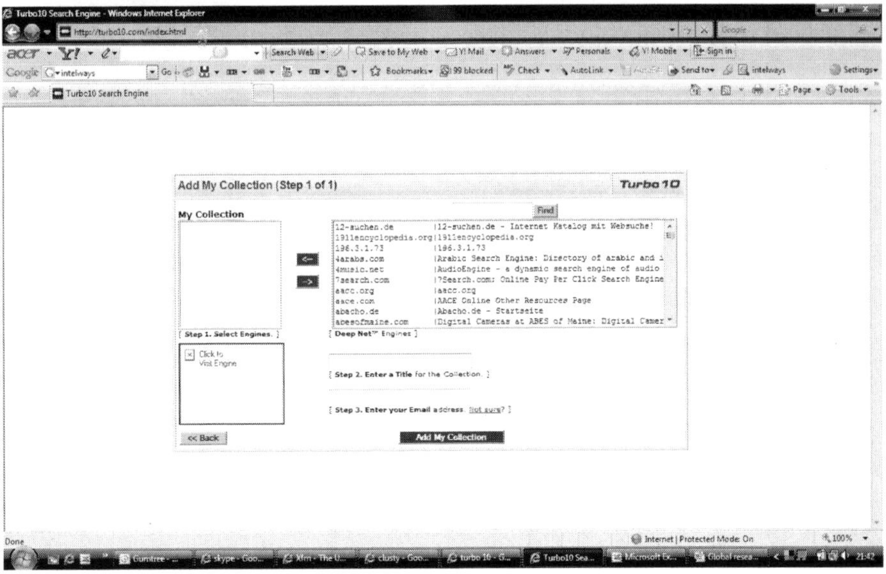

To select your own engine collections use the 'Add My Collection' section on the home page. See Figure 1.14.

### Exalead: *http://www.exalead.co.uk/search*

The left-hand side of the Exalead home page provides a visual display of the information found; on the right-hand side there is another clustering area to allow you to narrow your search using related terms, site type, multimedia, languages, directories and file types. See Figures 1.15 and 1.16.

### Cuil: *http://www.cuil.com/*

Cuil has recently arrived on the market. It provides searchers with a visual representation of the search results. It loads the pages very quickly, and seems to provide results that are relevant to what it has been asked for. Cuil has a good layout, displaying up to nine results per page plus a category section on the right of the screen to narrow the topic. See Figure 1.17.

### Trexy: *http://trexy.com/*

Megan Hamilton, joint-owner, describes Trexy in the following way:

> London based Trexy.com is the first search technology that enables users to remember and share search trails. A search trail is the path a user creates while searching and browsing the web. Trexy works

**Figure 1.15** Exalead search page

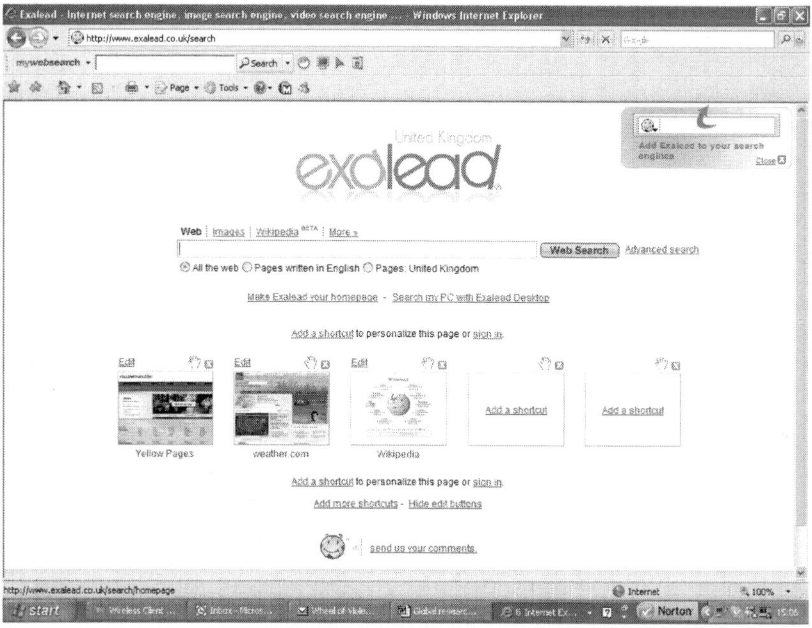

**Figure 1.16** Result of search on Exalead for 'commodities'

**Figure 1.17** Result of search on Cuil for 'derivatives'

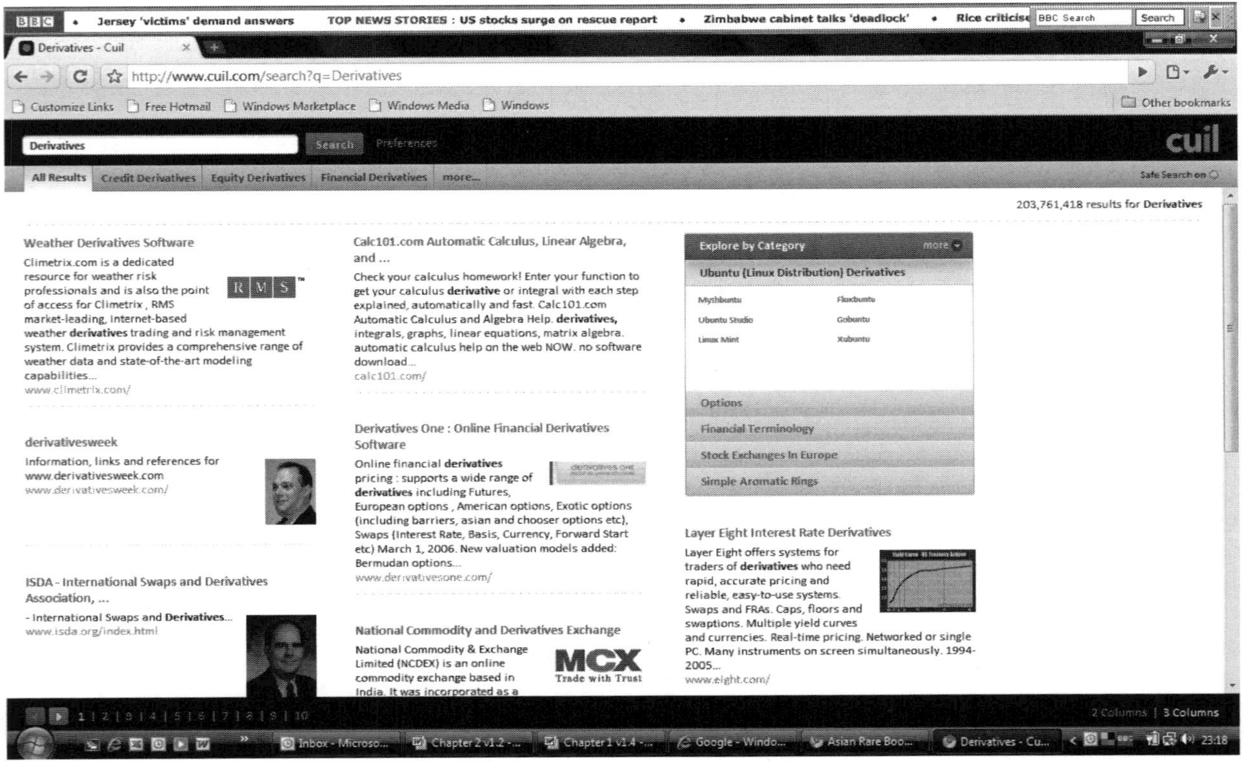

with over 4,000 online search engines and databases including Google, Yahoo and MSN.

Search trails are created by installing the free Trexy TrailButton™ that installs into Internet Explorer (5.0+) or Firefox (1.0+) web browsers.

The TrailButton tightly integrates with the web browser and detects HTML form submissions.

The 'Trailblazing On' light informs the user when they are trailblazing and the user can turn trailblazing off at any time. The unbroken sequence of links that the user follows while browsing the web for a solution forms the trail.

It is ultimately the user who decides the relevancy of a web page.

Trailblazing needs three things to work. First we need to navigate the 'common record.' Thanks to Ted Nelson's idea of hypertext, and Berners-Lee's implementation, the WWW provides an interlinked common record. Second, we need a way to remember useful trails of association through the common record. Third, the system should enable us to share our trails with others.

See Figure 1.18.

**Figure 1.18**   Trexy home page

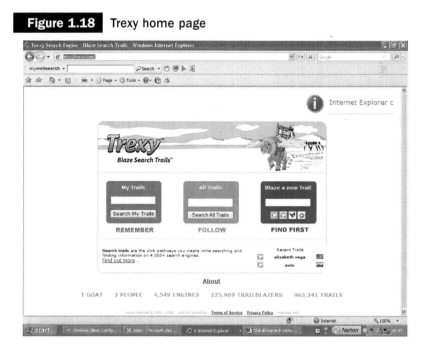

## All the Web: *http://www.alltheweb.com/*

Most search engines have a clean layout for ease of use, and All the Web is no exception. It has a new search option called LiveSearch for browsers running Javascript. See Figure 1.19.

**Figure 1.19** All the Web home page

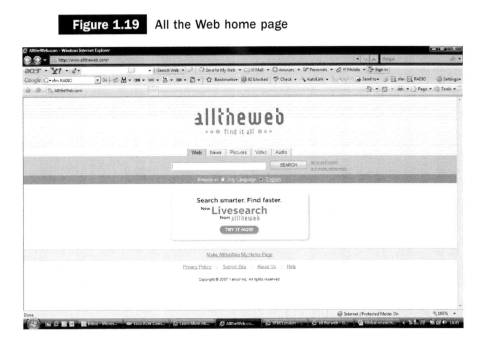

Twingine: *http://twingine.com/*

This was once called Yagoohoo!le in a former life, but it changed its name for obvious reasons. It is the creation of Norwegian Asgier S. Nilsen, who has a blog on the site. The main feature of this engine is that it has a dual screen and will return results from Yahoo! and Google on the same screen, which is great for making comparisons of your searches results! Figure 1.20 shows that there were sponsored links on the Yahoo! page and no sponsored links on the Google page for the search entered.

## Figure 1.20 Result of search on Twingine for 'foreign exchange laws malaysia'

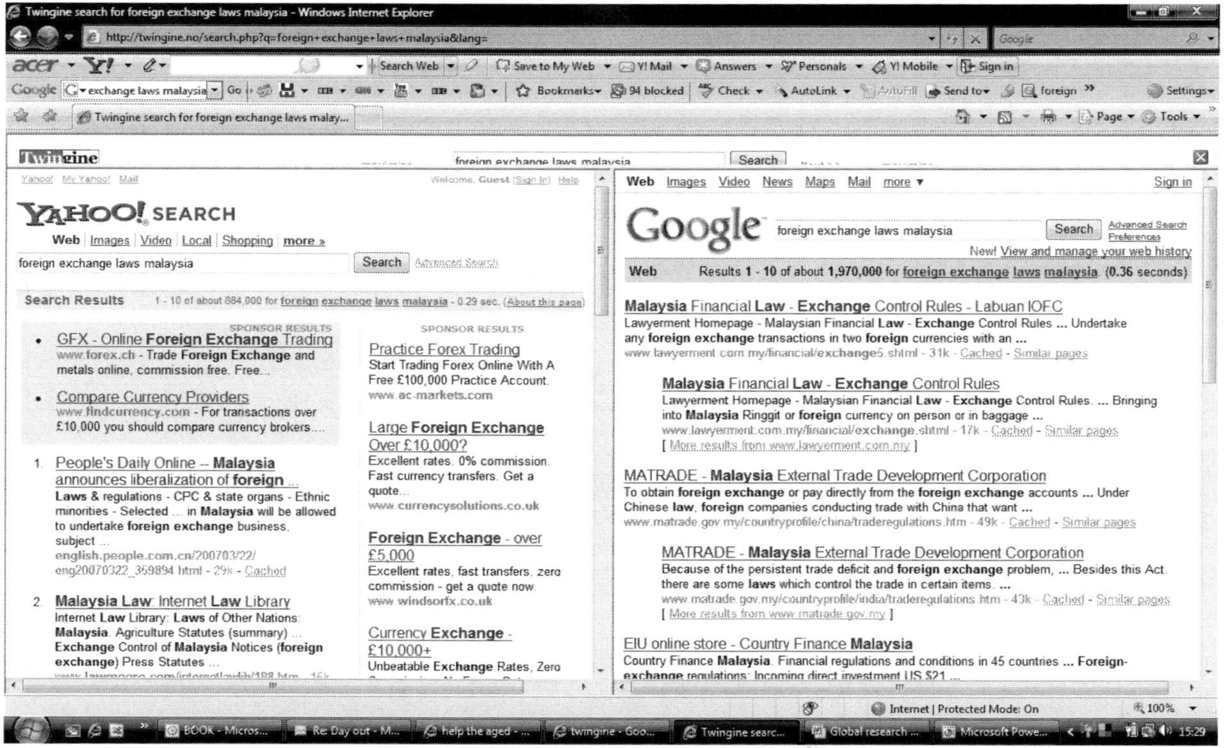

## Metasearch engines

Metasearch engines go through many different search engines at the same time and pull results into the same page, so one does not need to check different search engines separately. However, results are varied and can often be very hit and miss within the context of the original query.

We have mentioned Turbo 10 earlier, which allows you to select the engine(s) you wish to search, and then save them to your personal collection. Some other metasearch engines are discussed below.

### Intelways: http://www.intelways.com/ *Intelways*

Intelways has undergone a number of transformations, from Mr Sapo to CrossEngine and is now renamed Intelways. It is a useful tool; you can run one search and then click on the various tabs to locate information related to that topic from many different search engines. The screenshot in Figure 1.21 is a good example of what I found on the Internet Archive about the original Mr Sapo.

Intelways describes itself as a web search aggregator that can locate almost anything, including data from the deep web engines and online information providers. See Figure 1.22.

**Figure 1.21**  Result of search on Internet Archive for 'Mr Sapo'

**Figure 1.22** Intelways home page

SurfWax: *http://www.surfwax.com/*

SurfWax is a metasearch engine that uses nautical terminology to describe the services it offers. It has a very clean layout and search results are listed using a 'SnapSite' facility, title, source and statistical data (Figure 1.23). Jump on your surfboard and have a look.

**Figure 1.23** SurfWax home page

**Figure 1.24** Result of search on SurfWax for 'deep net'

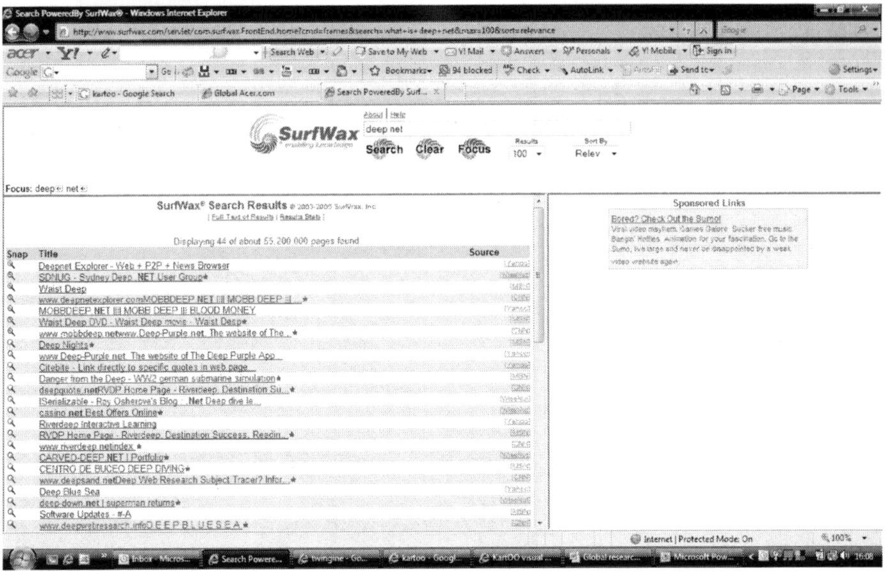

A search for 'deep net' pulled back results for: deep net fishing, Sydney deep.net user group, Turbo 10, mobbdeep.net, Deep Purple.net, tennis single maze and so on from Wisenut, MSN, CNN and Yahoo! (Figure 1.24).

These results were somewhat unexpected, but sometimes you literally get what you ask for if you don't ask the right question in the right context. See 'Bar orphans', an article I wrote for Freepint.[5]

## Dogpile: http://www.dogpile.com/

Dogpile covers Google, Yahoo!, Ask and more; the website explains the name:

> The time-saving philosophy of metasearch is so important to us that it even inspired our name! In rugby, players come together and pile on top of one another. This is exactly what Dogpile's metasearch technology does – it compiles all the best results in one easy-to-access place!
>
> And because every good team needs a loyal mascot, we adopted Arfie. You can find him any time on Dogpile, where he works as a retriever of sorts. When you search the Web on Dogpile, he's quick to fetch the exact results you want when you want them.

See Figures 1.25 and 1.26.

**Figure 1.25**  Dogpile home page

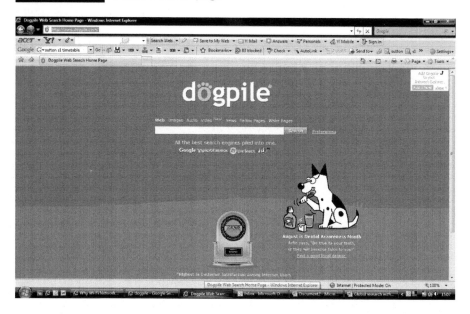

**Figure 1.26**  Result of search on Dogpile for 'commodities'

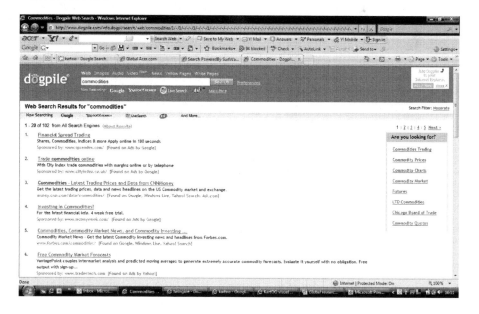

### Kartoo: *http://www.kartoo.com/*

Kartoo is a metasearch engine that provides a visual mind map to assist you in broadening or narrowing your search criteria. See Figure 1.27.

Figure 1.28 shows the results after searching on Kartoo for 'commodities'.

**Figure 1.27**    Kartoo home page

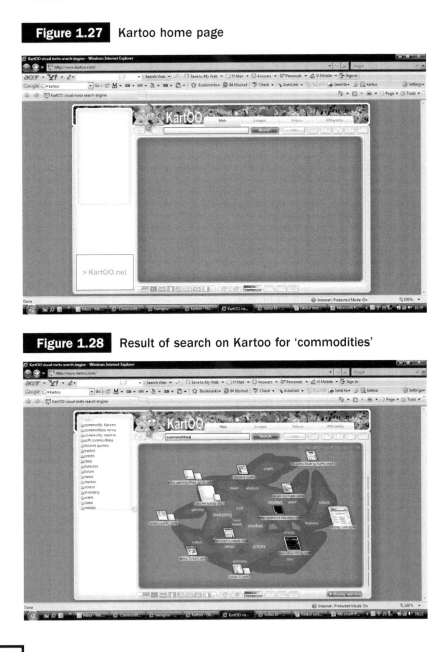

**Figure 1.28**    Result of search on Kartoo for 'commodities'

To the left hand of the page is a list of topics to broaden or narrow the search criteria. Click on one and the visual map will change accordingly. Kartoo has improved markedly in the last few years.

**Pagebull:** *http://www.pagebull.com/*

Pagebull is a visual search tool, which I located fairly recently. See Figure 1.29. A basic commodities search pulled in visual results from the FT, Financial News, Hemscott and Euronext, among other sites. It is set to display 12 web pages at a time, but one can view fewer or more frames if required. See Figure 1.30.

## Deep or invisible web resources

As spiders or bots are unable to index certain types of information; the data remains hidden in what is known as the deep or invisible web. The bots are unable to index the information because they cannot get past a password protected barrier and registration may be required to access the data; the pages may be encrypted so they cannot be indexed; or the information may be in a format the bots are unable to recognise in order to index it.

The way to access this information is to think about all types of databases and accessing them from corporate websites to higher

| Figure 1.29 | Pagebull home page |

**Figure 1.30** Result of search on Pagebull for 'commodities'

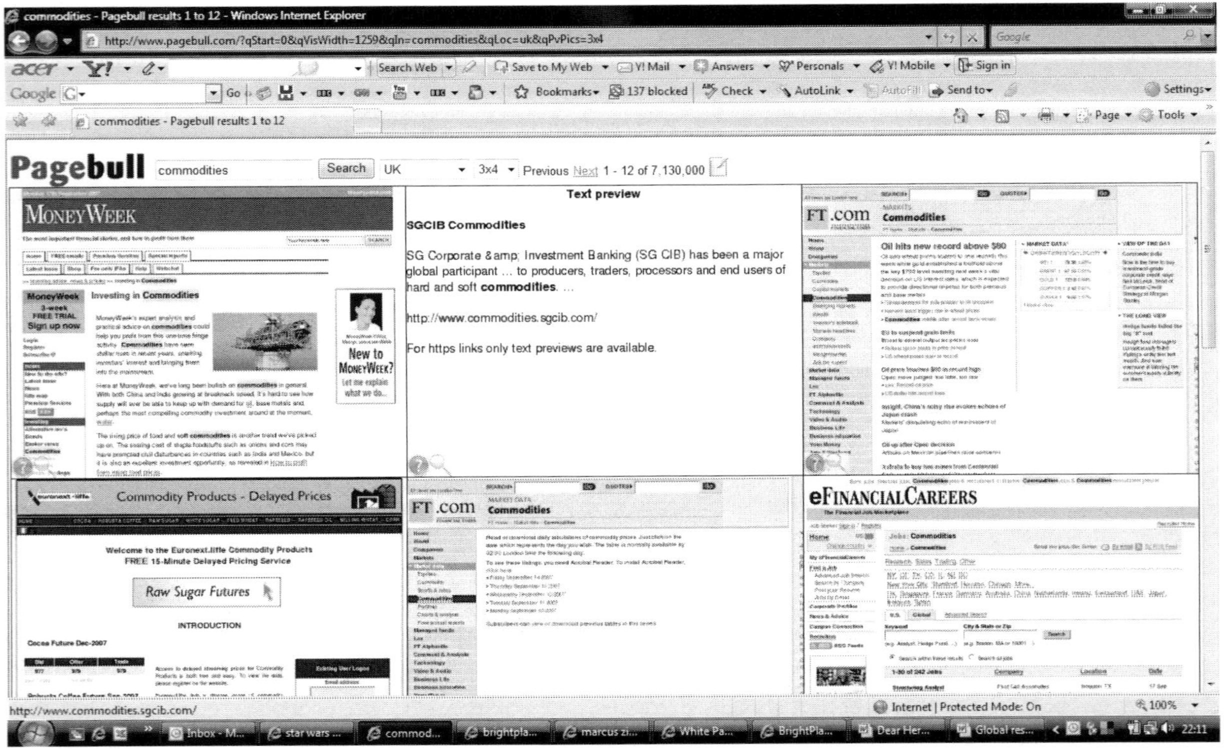

**Figure 1.31** Library Spot home page

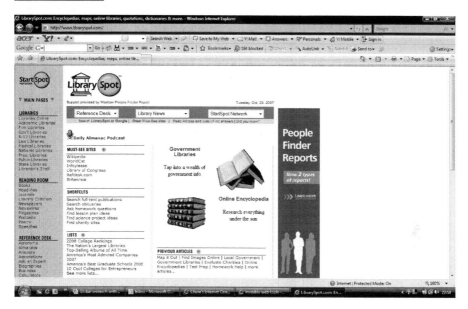

education. Most higher education institutions hold their own databases of information and these can be accessed by the general public in most instances. Some may require registration (paid or free) in advance of use. Many of the databases compiled by these institutions also act as gateways to other locations for finding specialist information.

### Library Spot: *http://www.libraryspot.com/*

Library Spot has a proliferation of information related to many different topics. It is somewhat US-centric, but the vast range of data held in Library Spot acts as a gateway to locating information in other regions outside the USA. See Figure 1.31.

### IncyWincy: *http://www.incywincy.com/*

IncyWincy will allow you to search the web, forms and images. See Figure 1.32. The directory tab points to a subject list. IncyWincy is an Open Directory Project where users are able to submit sites to the directory. There is also a section where users can submit their own website for inclusion in the directory.

Incy Wincy is a product of LOOP Improvements LLC (Figure 1.33).

**Figure 1.32** IncyWincy home page

**Figure 1.33** LOOP Improvements LLC home page

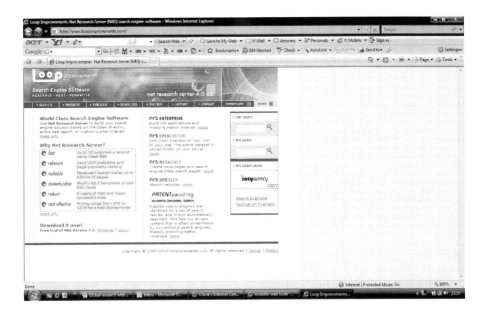

Robert J. Lackie's article 'Those dark hiding places' describes how one can access the hidden web (Figure 1.34).[6]

**Figure 1.34** Lackie's article 'Those dark hiding places' on his website

## The Ultimate Guide to the Invisible Web: *http://oedb.org/library/college-basics/invisible-web*

This Online Education Database (OEDb) takes a detailed look at the invisible web, and is worth reading. Check regularly on Ariadne, Pandia, FreePint and other information professional resources for updates on this topic, or load some alerts from discussion groups or RSS feeds for automatic alerts. This subject is of interest to many, therefore any new products or releases will be widely publicised in many mediums within the industry. Figure 1.35 shows the first page of the OEDb article on the invisible web.

## Marcus P. Zillman's blogspot: *http://marcuszillman.blogspot.com/*

Last in this section is the work of Marcus P. Zillman. I have been an avid reader of his work for many years. Scroll through his pages and see how many topics he covers. He just doesn't stop writing! Best of all, he provides access to many great ways to locate reliable free information. See Figure 1.36.

**Figure 1.35** Article 'The ultimate guide to the invisible web' on the Online Education Database

**Figure 1.36** The Marcus P. Zillman blogspot

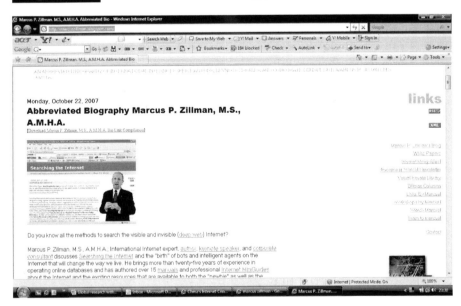

# Free or fee?

At what point would you think your time would be better spent using one of the proprietary databases to access the data you want? Time is money, so using a fee-based service has distinct advantages that you should bear in mind. Free or fee? Pre-formatted output by the service provider or corporate-defined deliverables? Another noticeable element to using the internet is that a lot of the good, reliable information that was previously freely available now requires payment. Researchers must find the balance, and train themselves to search proficiently on the fee-paying databases to keep search costs within budget for the cost centre or client.

## *Free stuff*

### From the subscripton-based services

In order to attract you to their websites in the first instance, providers of fee-paying services often offer free access to certain information. They want to ensure that you return for another visit, and maybe even purchase some services. Let's take a random look at what is on offer. When does a search engine become a subscription-based database service and does that concept work the other way round?

**Infovell: *http://www.infovell.com/index.shtml***

A company offering a new form of web search that offers deep web research has launched, offering quality, scholarly research – at a price. Infovell collaborates with a number of life sciences, medicines, patents and industry publishers to offer potential customers access to the content of millions of journal articles via those publishers. See Figure 1.37.

If this engine's target audience is the scientific research community, it limits its potential client audience, and it is unlikely that many business researchers would ever need to search by up to 25,000 'key phrases' or use highly complex mathematical equations.

Isn't this what the subscription-based services do by getting researchers to learn specific (simplified) search syntax, and aren't they web-based? Isn't a lot of the deliverable unavailable from a basic internet search, therefore requiring a deep web tool (think databases...)? Isn't the deliverable copyright protected, requiring licence fees for internal organisational distribution charged by user, cost centre or number of employees? Isn't the deliverable available in different languages and in customised formats that are tailored to clients' needs? Don't all these

**Figure 1.37** The Infovell home page

subscription-based services collaborate and swap data content to such an extent that the incestuous relationships built between them become so large that every service provider is offering everyone else's content, to maintain an 'edge' over their competitors?

I struggled to define any real differences between the products.

## Fee-paying resources

### All topics

#### Factiva: http://factiva.com/

Factiva is one of the industry's larger, high-quality, fee-based databases. If you pay a subscription, it would be easier to tell you what isn't covered in the way of data, except I haven't found out what isn't available. I am covering Factiva because of its free-trial access, which returns headlines only on all subjects, after which the researcher has the opportunity to search further on the internet. See Figure 1.38.

### Metals

#### Steel on the Net: http://www.steelonthenet.com

This site has a lot of free content. See Figure 1.39.

**Figure 1.38** Factiva home page

**Figure 1.39** Steel on the Net home page

## Oil and gas

**Alexander's Gas and Oil Connections:** *http://www.gasandoil.com/*

This has free content for the oil and gas industry including news headlines. See Figure 1.40.

# Figure 1.40 Alexander's Gas and Oil Connections home page

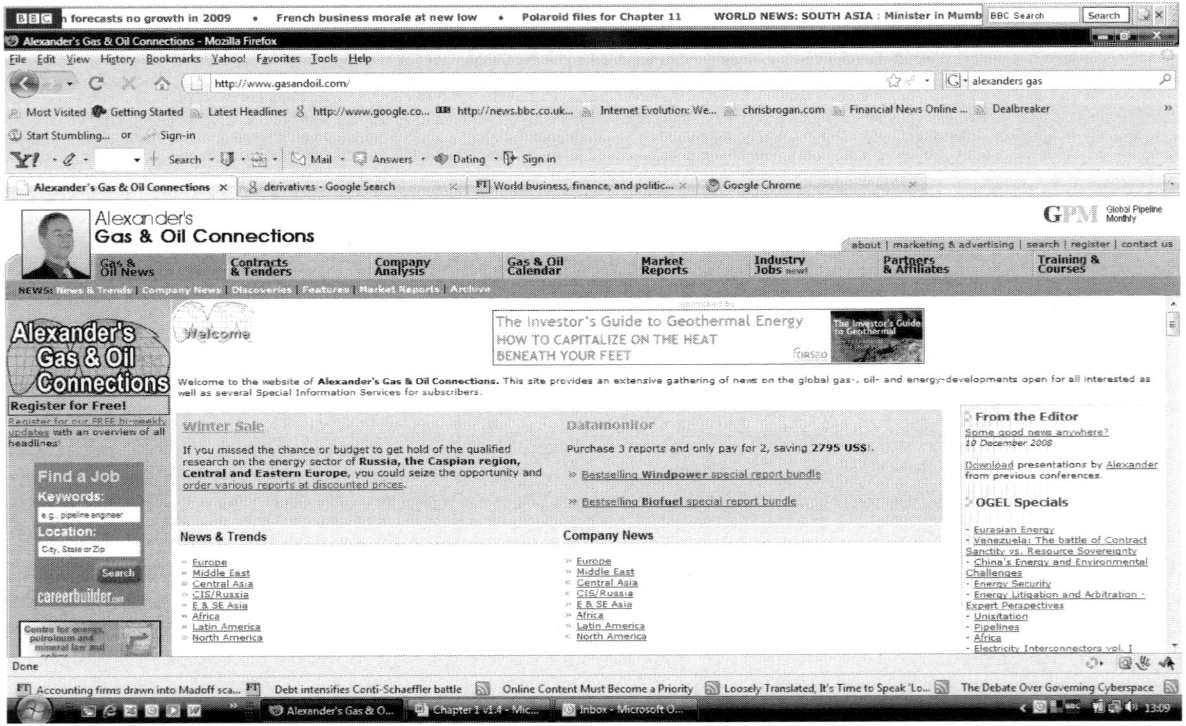

# Swaps and derivatives

### The International Swaps and Derivatives Association: *http://www.isda.org/index.html*

The International Swaps and Derivatives Association (ISDA) website provides free access to the latest news, surveys and markets statistical data and other information. See Figure 1.41. It points readers to other official portals such as the Office of the Comptroller of the Currency and the British Bankers' Association. The documentation that fee-paying members have access to is compiled by a consortium of top lawyers from the largest investment banks and law firms, who work as a committee to develop standard documentation specifically for use by the financial products industry. It is very expensive to use the standard documentation.

**Figure 1.41**   The ISDA website home page

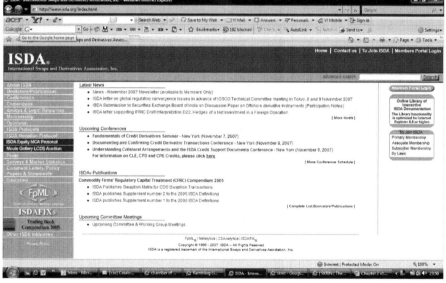

# Law

### Martindale.com: *http://www.martindale.com*

The Martindale.com site provides some free case law, forms and other resources via LexisNexis, but it is US-centric. Other offerings include directory listings. See Figure 1.42.

## Figure 1.42 The Martindale.com home page

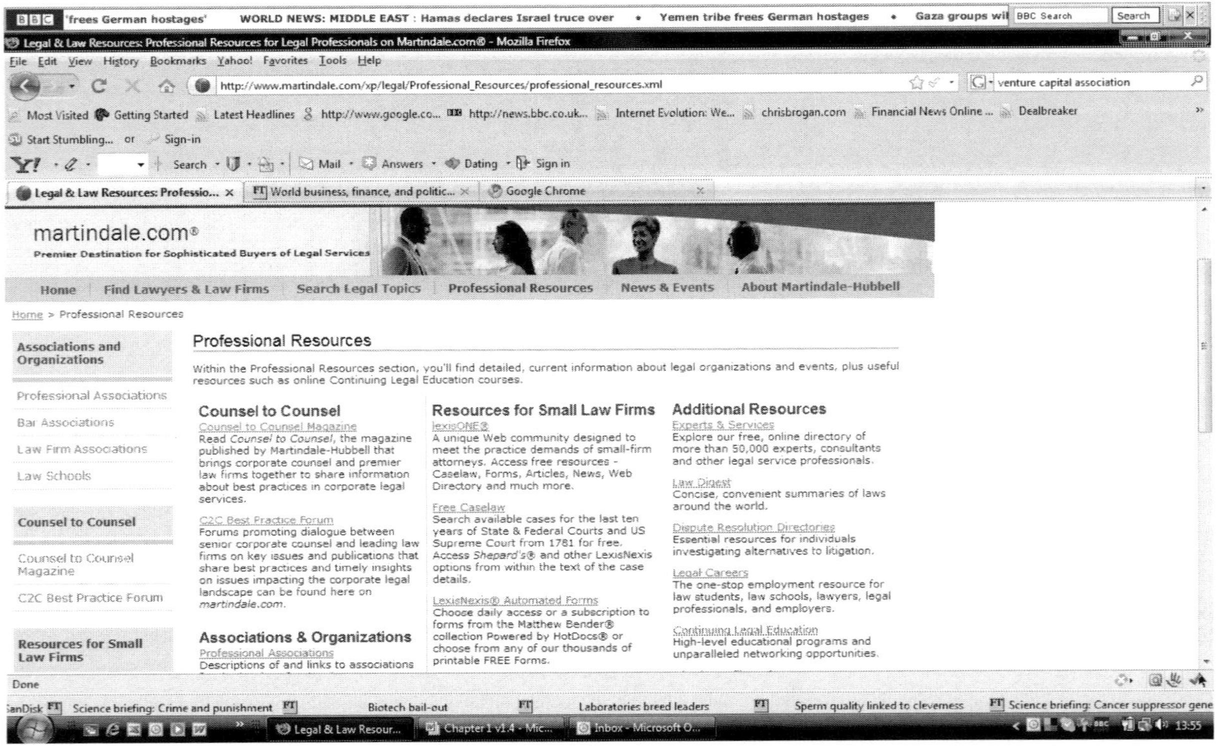

## Private and project finance

### The International Project Finance Association: *http://www.ipfa.org/index.shtml*

The International Project Finance Association website provides limited access for non-members to news, press releases and presentation materials. See Figure 1.43.

**Figure 1.43** The International Project Finance Association website home page

### Project Finance Magazine: *http://www.projectfinancemagazine.com/default.asp?page=8&sector=2*

This source provides free news headlines and the first few lines of the articles for free. RSS feeds are available. See Figure 1.44.

## Company information

These are just a few examples of the quality portals that can be easily located.

### Hemscott: *http://www.hemscott.com/companies/company-search.do*

Hemscott provides free basic company information, news, market data and newsletters. Previously known as Hemmington Scott, it has evolved into a sophisticated place to look for company data. See Figure 1.45.

**Figure 1.44** The Project Finance Magazine website home page

**Figure 1.45** Hemscott home page

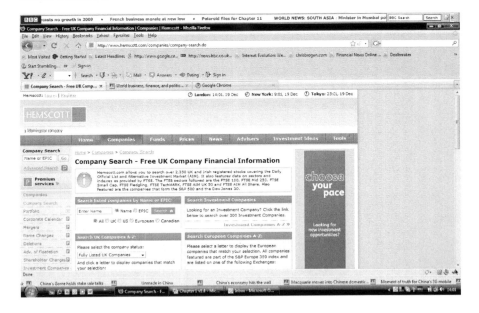

## CorporateInformation.com: *http://www.corporateinformation.com/*

This site has free snapshots of financial pages. See Figure 1.46.

**Figure 1.46** CorporateInformation.com home page

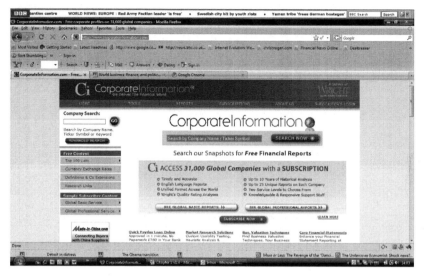

## SKRIN Russian Company Information: *http://www.skrin.com/*

This site provides free access to news, events, stock indices, industry sector data, enterprises and sectors, broker reports and statistics. See Figure 1.47.

**Figure 1.47** SKRIN home page

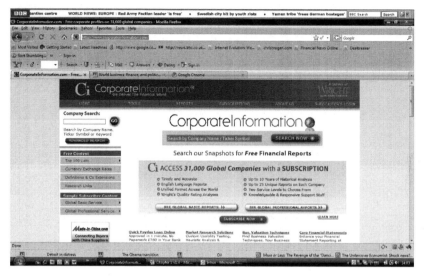

## Kompass: *http://www.kompass.co.uk*

Kompass allows users to drill down via the tabs and obtain basic company data from its website. See Figure 1.48.

**Figure 1.48** Kompass home page

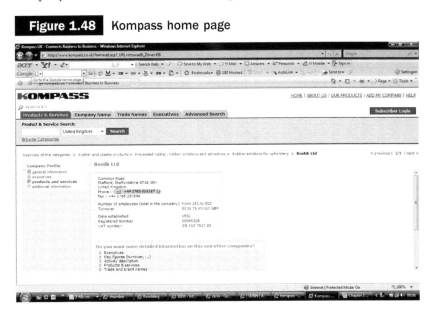

## Europa: *http://europa.eu/index_en.htm*

From the Europa website one can access all information for EU countries by industry, company, legislation, statistics, *Who's Who* and *Official Journal*.

**Figure 1.49** Europa home page

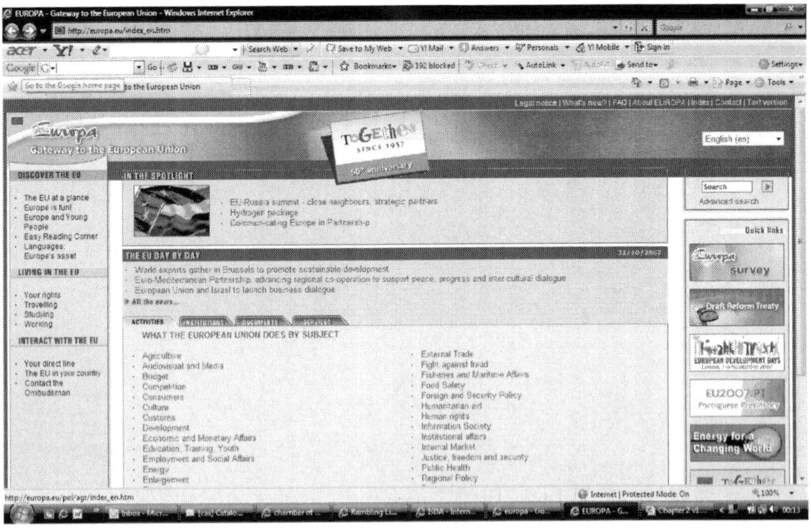

Information is provided in the language of every member country. See Figure 1.49.

**BRINT Institute:** *http://www.brint.org/#portals*

This resource is a think tank for business technology management and knowledge management. See Figure 1.50.

**Figure 1.50** Brint Institute home page

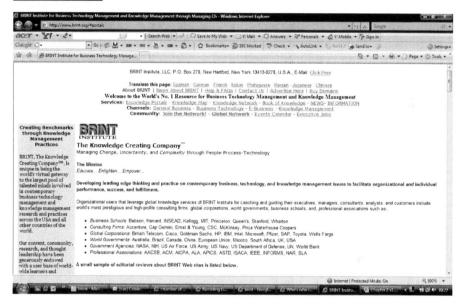

# List of websites mentioned in this chapter

About *http://websearch.about.com/library/tableofcontents/blsearch
enginetableofcontents.htm*
All the Web *http://www.alltheweb.com/*
Clusty *http://clusty.com/*
Cuil *http://www.cuil.com/*
Exalead *http://www.exalead.co.uk/search*
Firefox Search Cloudlet Add-on *http://www.getcloudlet.com/*
Google Cheat Sheet *http://www.google.com/help/cheatsheet.html*
Google Chrome *http://www.google.com/chrome*
Internet Archive: The WayBack Machine *http://www.archive.org/index.php*
OneLook *http://www.onelook.com/*

Pandia *http://www.pandia.com/*
Trexy *http://trexy.com/*
Turbo 10 *http://turbo10.com/searchthedeepnet.html*

## Metasearch sites

Dogpile *http://www.dogpile.com/*
Intelways *http://www.intelways.com/*
Kartoo *http://www.kartoo.com/*
Pagebull *http://www.pagebull.com/*
Surfwax *http://www.surfwax.com/*
Turbo 10 *http://turbo10.com/*
Twingine *http://twingine.com/*

## Deep or invisible web resources

IncyWincy *http://www.incywincy.com/*
Library Spot *http://www.libraryspot.com/*
Marcus P. Zillman's Blogspot *http://marcuszillman.blogspot.com/*
'Those dark hiding places: the invisible web revealed' by Robert J. Lackie, Ryder University *http://www.robertlackie.com/invisible/index.html*
'The ultimate guide to the invisible web' *http://oedb.org/library/college-basics/invisible-web*
Turbo 10 *http://turbo10.com/*

# Notes

1. Jason Prescott, 'B2B firms get niche targeting with vertical search engines', at *http://www.pandia.com/sew/361-vse.html*.
2. Wendy Boswell, '100 search engines in 100 days', at *http://websearch.about.com/library/tableofcontents/blsearchenginetableofcontents.htm*.
3. UC Berkeley, Finding Information on the Internet, 'Evaluating web pages: techniques to apply & questions to ask', at *http://www.lib.berkeley.edu/TeachingLib/Guides/Internet/Evaluate.html*.
4. Google Librarian Central, 'How does Google collect and rank results?', at *http://www.google.com/librariancenter/articles/0512_01.html*.
5. Jane Macoustra, 'Bar orphans: getting your questions answered at the FreePint Bar', at *http://web.freepint.com/go/newsletter/199#feature*.
6. Robert J. Lackie, 'Those dark hiding places: the invisible web revealed', at *http://www.robertlackie.com/invisible/index.html*.

# 2

# Global business information

In our research we never know what to expect before we set out: the research questions, and therefore the results, vary for different subjects. Sometimes you need country, regional and industry information to enable you to start your quest for gathering data from different angles to access the required information.

## General sources

You require some demographical information concerning the ageing population in a number of countries across more than one region. These statistics enable you to evaluate the requirements for life expectancy. You might need to analyse this sort of data if you are in the pensions industry or are working for the welfare of the elderly.

You could try Clusty (*http://clusty.com*; see Chapter 1, 'Tools and search engines, and their characteristics') and evaluate the clustered results (Figure 2.1). Notice that Wikipedia has dominant results on this page via the Clusty engine. However, being a sceptic, I don't use a wiki very often because the data can sometimes be manipulated by non-professionals. Writers of wiki entries can also be biased and instead of making an entry that is factual, neutral and accurate they make one that reflects their personal beliefs, so one questions why they have created a wiki entry in the first instance. If you look, you will find examples of wiki entries that are not pure fact. Be aware of them, and check other sources for accuracy, using scholarly gateways and reliable resources.

### Intute: *http://www.intute.ac.uk/*

Intute is a free online service funded by the Joint Information Systems Committee (JISC), and of high value and high quality. See Figure 2.2.

**Figure 2.1** Result of search on Clusty for 'demographics world comparison'

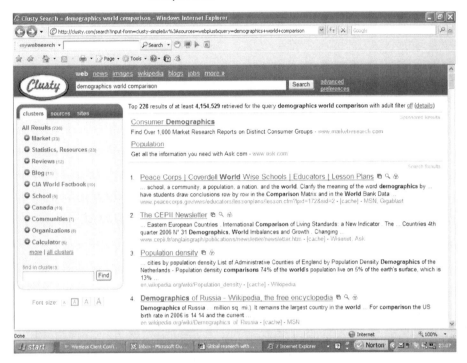

We selected the keywords Algeria, Canada, Hong Kong, Turkey and World to make a demographical comparison of life expectancy.

### The CIA World Factbook: *https://www.cia.gov/cia/publications/factbook/*

My mouse and I already knew that I could locate this demographical information via the CIA *World Factbook*, which is where this data originated from in the first instance. The advantage of using an online service is that if you know that the actual source is good you can then use the databases of the higher education systems to locate the same data. Then you can use their databases to run searches that will save you time and effort collating your data into predefined statistical formats, which you can use in your reports.

The *World Factbook* website is a constant companion for many people, whether conducting business research or helping children with their homework, such as teaching them about the differences between longitude and latitude, time zones and different climates or projects. It

### Figure 2.2    Intute statistics and data web page

contains a goldmine of free information and I constantly return to this resource. The Gutenberg Project is adding the CIA *World Factbook* to its collection of free books on the internet. See Figure 2.3.

### Figure 2.3    The CIA World Factbook 2007

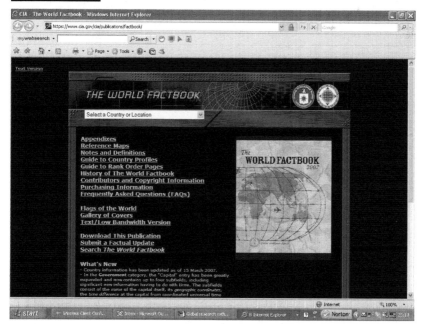

### Index Mundi: *http://www.indexmundi.com/world/demographics_ profile.html*

Index Mundi also takes its statistics from the CIA *World Factbook*, among other resources. It gives the last date that it was updated on each page. See Figure 2.4.

I executed a search for general world demographics. From the home page, click on a region and you can obtain data by country. There are charts and maps, commodities data and country facts supplied in a number of languages. Click on country rankings and access a page that allows you to gather statistical data by many different criteria. Correlation charts enable users to compile by topic of first and second variables. This is definitely worth a look.

### Silobreaker: *http://www.silobreaker.com/*

Another interesting database I'd like to point you at is Silobreaker. It is a commercial organisation, but it allows visitors to access certain types of data without payment. I like the features offered. Silobreaker is an aggregator with bolt-on additions, like some very fancy visual search features. Options include 360° Search, Network, Hot Spots and Trends, and there are blogs, news, factsheets and company profiles. There are many ways to search, so jump in and enjoy! The network search is

**Figure 2.4**  Index Mundi home page

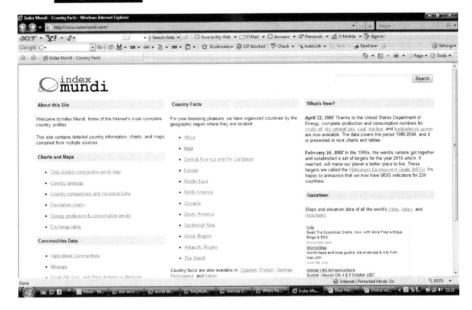

## Figure 2.5   Silobreaker home page

intriguing as the map is based on links to events, organisations and people. See Figure 2.5.

When searching for business information, don't forget the higher education institutions, where you will find lists of databases and resources for company information.

Notice how much information on a particular country or region is available from a global source or from a source in a completely different country or region.

### AllMyFaves: http://www.allmyfaves.com/

AllMyFaves is a colourful compilation of lots of websites that people often use. It's US/Canadian centric, but there are some sites you may never have seen before. Take the time to explore it. It's also a nice idea. See Figure 2.6.

There may be many places on the planet that we haven't visited before, but one way to take a look around is by using Google Earth, which launched version 5.0 in summer 2009. Google Earth now offers more ways to view the earth, and more ways to manage the folders of places visited. See Figure 2.7.

**Figure 2.6** AllMyFaves home page

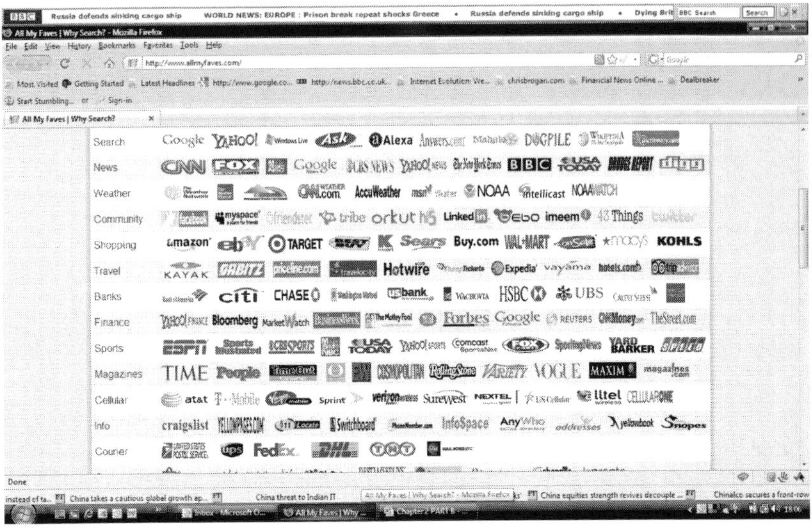

Google Earth will 'fly' you around the world to any place you name and give you various options, including recording your tour, placemarking, historical imagery and a view of sunlight over the landscape. There are detailed instructions for using this tool for fun or

**Figure 2.7** Google Earth home page

business purposes at Google Earth User Guide (*http://earth.google .com/intl/en_uk/userguide/v4/#fivethings*). I am aware of the other uses for this tool, and hope that Google will 'monitor' where people visit since we already know it happens.

Privacy International (*http://www.privacyinternational.org/*) was formed in 1990 to monitor surveillance and privacy invasions by governments and corporations.

## Using local knowledge

When you are on unfamiliar territory, sometimes the best way to locate information is to use local knowledge. Use local search engines to locate local content.

Be aware that use of a local search engine can mean that the data retrieved may be censored, so a comparison is necessary to ascertain what you aren't seeing. Compare local searches with global ones to ensure that you get a balanced return of results. For example, the subject of baby milk contamination in China and the surrounding areas was censored on Baidu, the largest Chinese search engine. Be aware of negative press that may be removed for political or business purposes and locate it elsewhere, so you see both sides of a story.

Local searching cannot be ignored as part of the research trail. The *Financial Times* published an article called 'Google still struggling to conquer outposts',[1] demonstrating that local searching was holding its own in certain parts of the world and that Google had struggled to gain a grip in some countries.

### Search Engine Colossus: *http://www.searchenginecolossus.com/*

Search Engine Colossus lists search engines by country. After clicking on a country, the list of search engines has a country of origin, which is an indication of where the information might have been indexed. It also gives you the language that the search engine uses. Not all of them are in English. See Figure 2.8.

### DMOZ The Open Directory Project: *http://www.dmoz.org/ Regional/*

DMOZ also has a search engine listing by region or continent, which is then sub-categorised by country and subject. See Figure 2.9.

**Figure 2.8**  Search Engine Colossus home page

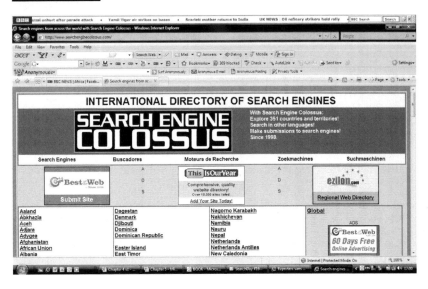

**Figure 2.9**  Open Directory Project home page

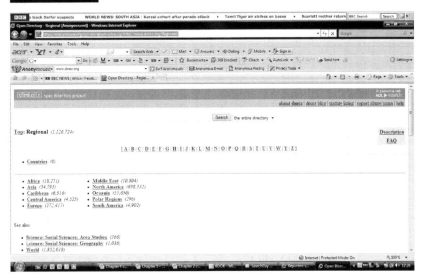

Craigslist: *http://www.craigslist.org/about/*

Craigslist is an online community that provides classified listings and discussion forums in more than 500 cities over 50 countries. The forums are moderated and the content is free. It covers many different topics and gives access to local businesses. See Figure 2.10.

**Figure 2.10**   The 'About craigslist' page on Craigslist

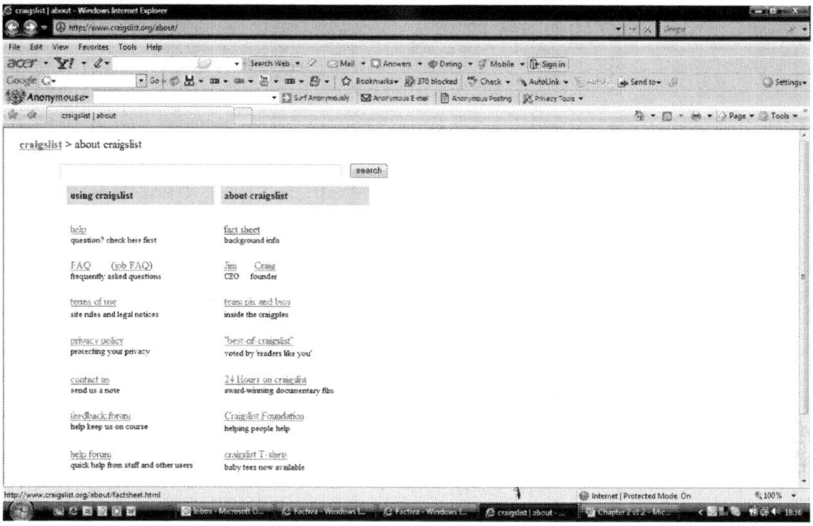

In Chapter 4, 'Terrorism, surveillance and corruption', we will be looking at corruption indices. If you or your organisation are thinking of doing business research anywhere, and are unfamiliar with the territory, check Transparency International (*http://www.transparency.org*) if there is any doubt about the country or the industry you are researching.

Consider the pros and cons of searching by country or continent, or globally. Look for international trade journals and use their RSS feeds to stay updated about new developments in your areas of interest. Locate relevant industry portals as they will cover global industries, which you break down to your specific requirements.

## *Currency converters*

How far back can you trace the history of the currency exchange of the Algerian Dinar? At the time of writing, £1 is worth DZA130.52. I used CoinMill.com (*http://coinmill.com/*) for a currency converter, as it covers many of the smaller currencies from African nations and checked other converters to try and get historical rates. In 1995 the Dinar was exchangeable at 39.25 to £1 and in 1994 it was 36.08. I could not go back any further using a free service. (See Figure 2.11.) Other currency converters that went back further, for example Oanda (*http://www .oanda.com/*), did not recognise the Algerian Dinar as an exchangeable currency.

**Figure 2.11** Conversion rates for the Algerian Dinar on CoinMill.com

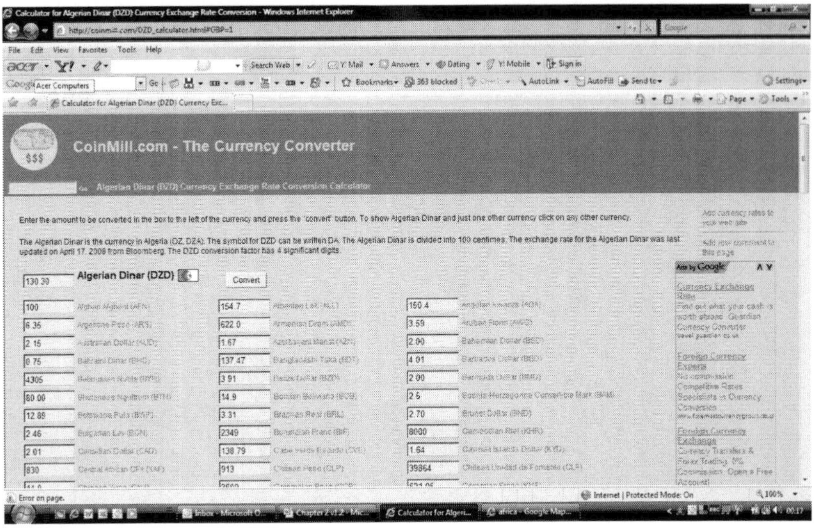

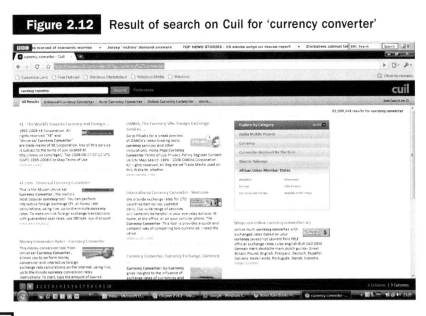

See also xrates.com (*http://www.x-rates.com/cgi-bin/hlookup.cgi*).

Currency forecasts are available for the Algerian Dinar from the Economist Intelligence Unit at *http://www.eiu.com/index.asp?layout= VWArticleVW3&article_id=1852967770&region_id=&country_id= 210000021&channel_id=200004020&category_id=&refm=vwCh&page_ title=Article&rf=0.*

**Figure 2.12** Result of search on Cuil for 'currency converter'

Figure 2.12 shows the result of a search on Cuil (*http://www.cuil .com/search?q=currency%20converter*) for currency converters.

## Maps and directories

Maps are a good way of gathering data, including historical data. Technological advancements using satellite imagery and global positioning systems allow researchers to use maps to evaluate communications, pipelines, trade and shipping routes. Maps also allow us to follow global human migration, political, economic and cultural data.

Directories are another way to locate organisations, and there are plenty of them freely available. The European Association of Directory and Database Publishers (see below) is a good place to start. There are many electronic directories which will allow free searches, including Yellow Pages, White Pages, Hoover's, Europages and Kompass.

**The European Association of Directory and Database Publishers:**
**http://www.eadp.org/index.php?q=DIRECTORIES**

The European Association of Directory and Database Publishers (EADP) website has lists of directories covering all industries and regions. The website is searchable by general subject, specialised subject or telecommunication type, and it includes regional and local directories. See Figure 2.13.

**Figure 2.13**  The EADP website home page

# Country information

## Europe

There are 27 member countries of the European Union (EU) and a lot of information on these countries is available through EU websites.

### Europa: *http://europa.eu/*

Much data can be captured from the EU website Europa, which has a monolith of data, and has become much more user friendly over the years. Choose your language and off you go. See Figure 2.14.

Europa is a gateway to all things EU. There are four main tabs on the page: for Activities (subject index), Institutions (agency, financial, interinstitutional, decentralised and advisory), Documents (everything available including the legal database) and Services (teaching, statistics, press room, library and lots more).

The legal database is EUR-Lex, at *http://eur-lex.europa.eu*. The official source for public contracts in Europe is Ted (tenders electronic daily), at *http://ted.europa.eu*. The latest news about R&D in the EU is available at *http://cordis.europa.eu*. Finally, Eurostat has the statistical databases at *http://epp.eurostat.ec.europa.eu/portal/page/portal/statistics/themes*; they are very detailed! They have a metadata section for standard classification by theme, structure, standard code lists and glossary and thesauri – a cataloguers' heaven!

**Figure 2.14** Europa home page

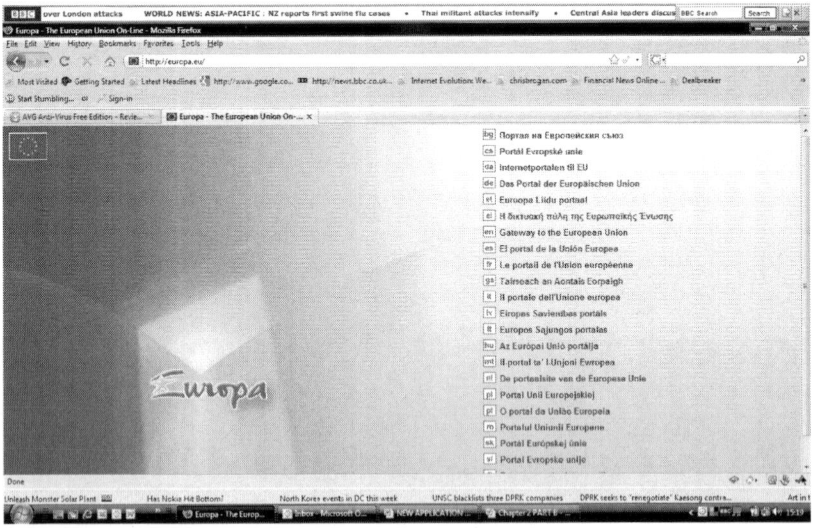

## England

England's main areas of business are banking and finance, insurance, tourism and the services industries, so let's take an easy stroll through the City of London. The Square Mile is very beautiful and oozes history, culture and tradition from every nook and cranny.

I experienced the Big Bang in the City. This was new regulatory legislation that changed the way the stock markets and financial world operated, instigated by the Thatcher government in the 1980s. I also remember the weak fizzle of Y2K in 2000, when everyone (even the airlines!) was afraid the electronic financial system would fail on the stroke of midnight of the new millennium.

In the past I was an avid reader of books about the financial world, *Barbarians at the Gate, Big Bets Gone Bad, Making it Happen, Slater Walker* and *Rogue Trader* being just a few I selected.[2] I especially enjoyed the scandals and somewhat dodgy tactics used to attempt to remedy dangerous financial situations or be the winner in huge complex deals.

Satyajit Das was a rocket scientist whose work I first came across in the 1980s. At the time, Das was writing for *International Financing Review* and I regularly read his column – in hard copy of course! He's been writing in the investment banking world for a long time and I was pleased to stumble over his blog 'Fear and loathing in financial products'. His comments on credit default swaps were a revelation and included commentary from other Masters of the Financial Universe about where they think the credit default swaps and derivatives market has ended up or may end up soon.[3] There's a quote at the beginning that is particularly poignant: 'As former New York Federal Reserve President Gerald Corrigan told policy-makers and financiers on 16 May, 2007: "Anyone who thinks they understand this stuff is living in lala land."'

When deals go wrong the lawsuits that follow can get dirty. But they can also result in some precedent-setting legislation that governs those who follow in their steps. Hazell v Hammersmith and Fulham London Borough Council (1992) House of Lords was one of those cases. It changed the world of interest rate swaps when it was decided that Hammersmith and Fulham did not have the legal capacity (it was *ultra vires* and therefore unlawful) to enter into interest rate swaps with a counterparty. History was made in the legal world with this particular case.

In summer 2009 it is still not clear how many borough councils lost money in Icelandic banks and if they can't retrieve their money what type of lawsuits follow if they didn't do their know your customer (KYC) credit checks properly and retained supporting documentation?

England's manufacturing industry has taken a massive hit in the economic downturn and is on the verge of collapse. Any recent newspaper will give you this information with appropriate graphs. Manufacturing portals have professional gateways where you can obtain statistical data to back up data reported in the press. The difference is that the industry won't mention the word 'collapse', when the press will.

PricewaterhouseCoopers (PwC; *http://www.pwc.com/*) has a number of publications available on the manufacturing industry for the UK and globally. See Figure 2.15.

There is a prolific amount of data on UK tourism available from a website called VisitBritain.org (*http://www.visitbritain.org/*), previously TourismTrade.org.

The Visit Britain business section requires payment to access data. Some of the data is drawn from the IMF *World Economic Outlook Report 2009*. The key tourism facts are basic, and key tourism trends are up to date so there's a huge amount of free data on this site covering accommodation and employment statistics, and other industry groups and bodies. See Figure 2.16.

**Figure 2.15** Information about manufacturing on the PricewaterhouseCoopers website

**Figure 2.16** Visit Britain web pages on insight and market intelligence on TourismTrade.org

## France

France has a lot of industry; two of the main ones are refining and metals. By searching maps for French refineries, it is possible to get a basic visual representation of where the refineries are located in France and who the operators are, including contact details. See Figure 2.17.

**Figure 2.17** Result of a search on Google Maps for 'france refining industry'

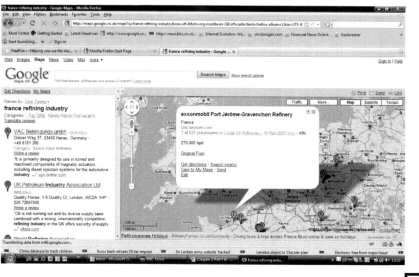

## Sweden

Sweden is cold in the north and warmer in the south, and some of its industries include pulp and paper, mining, telecommunications and water. It is a member of the EU.

### Statistics Sweden: *http://www.ssd.scb.se/databaser/makro/start.asp?lang=2*

The Statistics Sweden website is a set of agricultural databases that can be accessed freely unless you require a customised search. Key indicators are available from the news and press pages and RSS is offered to load into your browser. See Figure 2.18.

Other interesting places I found included a Viking database, Swedish law on the internet, a venture capital directory in Sweden and more.

## The Russian Federation

The Russian Federation is the largest country in the world, and has extremes of temperatures from its freezing north to its warm southerly climate where it borders onto Asia. It's got the deepest lake in the world – the Baikal. It has many different industries, including energy, mining, precious metals, pulp and paper and manufacturing. Its agricultural

**Figure 2.18**  'Finding statistics' on the Statistics Sweden website

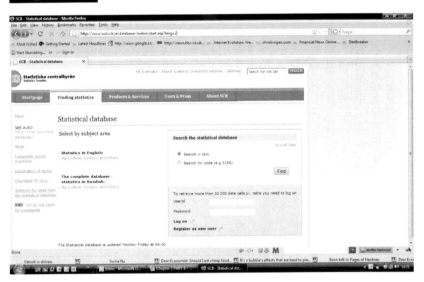

industry is not great due to the climate, so a number of foods, such as grain, are imported. Information about the Russian Federation is easily available in English.

### Russian Law News: *http://www.russianlaws.com/resources/*

Dewey & LeBouef provides access to some very decent data on Russian company information, legislation, agencies, bibliographies and miscellaneous hyperlinks at Russian Law News. See Figure 2.19.

There are quite a few databases available on the Russian Federation; however you need to find ones that will allow English language access, and to check the last time the website was updated. The Virtual Library on Agriculture – in Russian – appears not to have been updated since 2002.

### AgroWeb Russian Federation: *http://www.cnshb.ru/aw/.%5Cshow .asp?page=sci\iv*

AgroWeb Russian Federation site has lists of many organisations related to a variety of different industries (Figure 2.20).

Data can also be obtained from the CIA *World FactBook*, the OECD, IMF and other organisations already mentioned.

There are research papers available such as this one on the pulp and paper industry by Professor Eduard L. Akim (Figure 2.21).[4] This detailed document provides statistical data and mentions who's who in the

---

**Figure 2.19** 'Resources' on Russian Law News

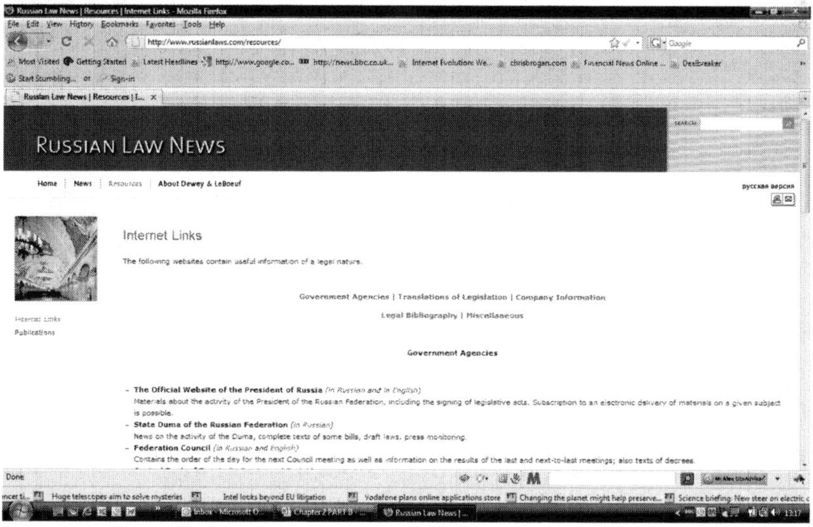

**Figure 2.20** AgroWeb Russian Federation site list of institutes

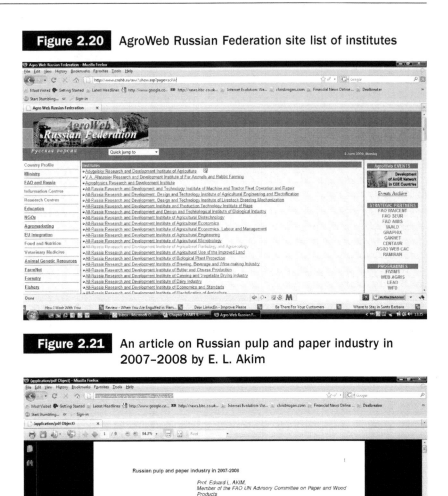

**Figure 2.21** An article on Russian pulp and paper industry in 2007–2008 by E. L. Akim

industry. Policy developments for 2004–2008 were to include the use of satellite surveillance to prevent illegal timber cutting.

### ArcheoBiblioBase: *http://www.iisg.nl/abb/*

The International Institute of Social History's (IISG's) ArcheoBiblioBase is an archive of records in the Russian Federation pre-2004 data. These archives include records on the arts and literature, military, navy, sound recordings, photography, foreign affairs and the State Atomic Energy Corporation. This is just a tiny selection of what is available, so whether you are an atomic scientist or a social scientist this set of databases is worth knowing about. See Figure 2.22.

| Figure 2.22 | IISG's ArcheoBiblioBase |

# Africa

The African continent is a challenging region to research, because of a lack of transparency in market, business, statistical and financial data. It is difficult to verify the accuracy of the information gathered, and the official source of that information.

When undertaking research for this book I located what appeared to be some good reliable data – until I hit the discussion forums. One particular financial website looked as though it was providing professional research tools. However, it had some very unprofessional discussion forums. Beware. Would you really use data from a provider who has unmoderated discussion lists and allows inappropriate content to be posted? This was no error on the part of the provider, where one or two postings had sneaked in; the postings were prolific. I was dismayed to see that a well-known university was actually listing this particular website as a reliable source of financial information for use by its students.

Ensure you explore these sites in greater detail (yes – I know that's a conflicting suggestion!) before ever attempting to use the data provided and step away as soon as you verify the data is of poor quality. Just because it is free – or even paid for – does not mean it is of good quality. Allowing access to financial data may be a thinly veiled façade to entice the uninitiated into areas of dubious content.

I checked the Namibian Stock Exchange website to ascertain the extent of inappropriate content on business websites in the region, and wasn't particularly surprised to see a pop-up with a woman in a bikini gracing the screen. At this point my laptop took exception to this content and blocked the rest of the pop-ups and other content, so I deleted my entire browsing history and files before continuing on my journey. It is a good idea also to reboot your internet connection when getting into areas such as these if you are not anonymising your searches by using a barrier host as your intermediary.

Finally I took a look at Namibia Financial Institutions Supervisory Authority (NAMFISA) (*http://www.namfisa.com.na*) to ascertain the independent status of this financial regulator. It only regulates the non-banking financial industry and is funded by the companies it regulates. Unfortunately, as with some – but not all – of the African internet infrastructure, the web servers and websites don't always work, and this was a prime example. Accessing information was painfully slow or the servers timed out before the pages could open. Searching local business directories in the area did not provide many results.

## Rwanda

In Rwanda internet blogs and articles abound of an internet revolution happening there. This seemed a strange occurrence for a country that has been in turmoil, experiencing unrest and genocide in recent years and required further exploration.

Internet Evolution produced an informative video called *Rwanda's Internet Evolution*, presented by Stephen Saunders (*http://www .internetevolution.com/document.asp?doc_id=168518*). The film describes Rwanda's ambitious plans for a knowledge-based economy in sub-Saharan Africa, detailing the rebuilding of its infrastructures and large investment costs. Students from the Kigali Institute of Science and Technology talk about what they are learning and their use of the internet to access information and knowledge. Wireless internet access is free wherever you go, and 75 per cent of schools are internet enabled.

In the Congo there is another revolution happening where the internet is flourishing via the use of mobile phones, with 3.2 million mobile phone users, and a growing market of 8,000 per day. Stephen Saunders notes that the future of the internet is in Africa.[5] This is a region that shouldn't be ignored as a possible future powerhouse.

## South Africa

A good way to access information in nations that are difficult to explore is to use a government portal. The information has passed through the hands of an information professional, who has reviewed the data for accuracy before putting it into the public domain.

**Portals to the World:** *http://www.loc.gov/rr/international/portals .html*

The Library of Congress provides a global gateway to portals of the world. From here you can search by country and region; for example, information on South Africa is at *http://www.loc.gov/rr/international/ amed/southafrica/resources/southafrica-search.html* (Figure 2.23). This site has lists on many subjects including government, acts and legislation, education and cultural studies, and includes business directories, newsletters, a reading room and special reports in French and English.

**Figure 2.23** Information on South Africa on Portals to the World

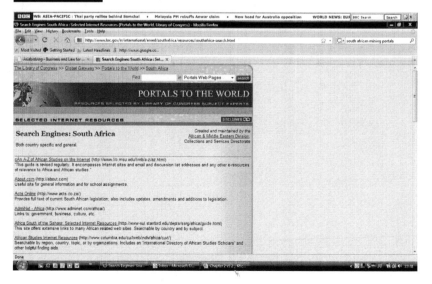

Many African countries are covered and the data is updated regularly by the Collections and Services Directorate.

## Intute: *http://www.intute.ac.uk*

On the Intute website, a general search for information on the African mining industry points to authors, organisations and other bodies where you can go to locate unbiased, objective information.

## MBendi: *http://mbendi.co.za/index.htm*

MBendi is a reliable portal for business information, which claims to be Africa's leading business and travel website. It offers a free newsletter, access to business opportunities, directories and news subscriptions.

The search can be narrowed down by many types of mining such as bauxite, gold, diamonds, heavy minerals, molybdenum, and geophysical surveying and mapping. A search on gold mining displayed results by providing a brief overview of gold mining in Africa, a very short summary for each country, and a list of gold mining companies and operators. Although this isn't hugely detailed, it's enough to start off a map of who, what and where, which can be built on with further research.

Click on the company hyperlinks and receive company information including communication details, a list of directors, business sectors and products and services. If you want more information you can obtain it

**Figure 2.24** Mbendi home page

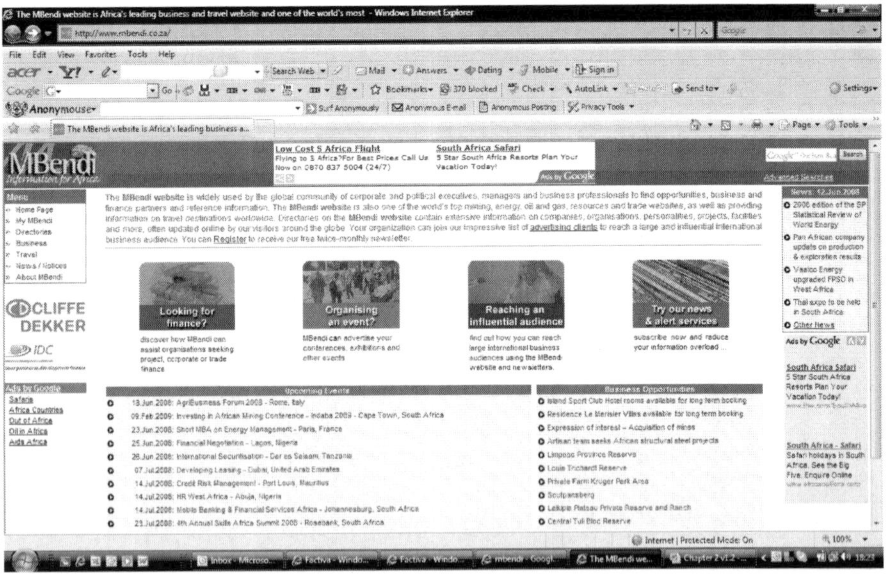

on payment of a fee. Remember to check when the site was last updated. See Figure 2.24.

Another way to explore African nations is to check out the websites of business councils, the World Bank and other officially recognised organisations. Kenya brings thoughts of heat, dust, the Masai Mara tribal people and the friendliness they offer to a visitor. You can explore the Kenyan business world via their newspapers, but the discussion forums I accessed via a business centre were not always recently updated, indicating a fragmented technological infrastructure or one that was at least intermittent for the user. I located a forum with a list of the richest people in Kenya on the Mashada discussion forum (*http://www.mashada .com/forums/general-discussion/66919-list-kenya-s-richest.html*).

Superdirectories.com (*http://www.superdirectories.com/?Branch_ID= 551319*) is an American organisation providing global resources that have been edited by people, not machines. Here you can search a huge range of subjects by country.

### Business Daily: *http://www.bdafrica.com/*

*Business Daily* is an African daily newspaper. See Figure 2.25.

The African Studies Centre at the University of Pennsylvania (*http://www.africa.upenn.edu/asc/bussguide.html*) offers a directory of African business resources.

**Figure 2.25** Home page of the Business Daily website

The Nairobi Stock Exchange (*http://www.nse.co.ke/newsite/index .asp*), although small, seems to have the requisite attributes expected of a regulatory system whose main activity is the trading of equities and bonds.

## The Middle East and Asia

In 2009 the Middle East business and investment markets are moving faster than one can keep up with. Large corporations are now tapping this region for funds in the wake of the current economic crisis, and despite a lack of general public knowledge of this region, the business professionals have the knowledge to complete these complicated cross-border deals.

Large swathes of land and property are being bought out all over the world by the Middle East, and Asian businesses and the global picture map of power, control and financial (in)stability is changing radically in a short space of time. As these economic powerhouses alter, we see a new takeover bid for domination by those who have waited patiently, watching as the global economy quietly unravels itself – only just under the control of the central banking systems.

The contributors to these changes are counterparty defaults in the (credit) derivatives markets, followed by economic crashes and bankruptcies, now supported by those who have the money to buy into distressed economies, countries, organisations and industries. The distressed or toxic debts accrued explode, systemically crushing, bringing everything down with them in their path like a volcano. Meltdown is indeed the best description for the destruction that still occurs. The vulture funds were waiting for them and no region is unaffected by these changes in the global economy.

Looking east, you need to locate the latest financial statistical data for the financial markets in Asia, excluding Japan. Where would you begin to look? Who would be the key holder of this kind of data without resorting to a proprietary database?

There is more than one Silk Road to stroll down to locate the required information. Think laterally about who would have this information. A regulator, perhaps, or maybe a stock exchange? It is possible but it may not be in English. But then if you want Asia excluding Japan, one regulator may only have the information for one country. So would you go to each country's financial regulatory website? The answer is yes and no. How about a global governing board that might collect this data and compile their own reports for the finance industry? There are many places to dig in, so don't restrict your search to just one or two sites; look at other sites and make comparisons of the data available and check the timeliness of that information.

# Israel

### Info-Prod Research (Middle East) Ltd: *http://www.infoprod.co.il/ about.htm*

When I researched this site I found it had not been updated since 2002, and includes a quote from the *Wall Street Journal* of 1993. There is a gaming machine at the bottom of the screen and the site appears to be based in Israel. Info-Prod seems to have impeccable alliances with the big service providers, but this is your wake up call... No matter where you are in the world, you would expect to see relevant amendments to business ethics, legislation and regulation in the financial markets. The business markets would be expected to evolve in combination with developments in other nations with regard to economic conditions, and substantive regulatory and legislative changes, such as Sharia legislation. Further investigation demonstrated that many other pages on the website had not been amended since 1999 – for 10 years. See Figure 2.26.

**Figure 2.26** 'About IPR' on Info-Prod Research (Middle East) Ltd

### Israel Science and Technology: http://www.science.co.il/

A further search for portals led to the website of the Israel Science and Technology. This site is properly copyrighted, up to date, and has a clean, professional look with information listed by subject, organisation and funds. A look at the news sources provided information in English, Hebrew, French and Russian, listing newspapers, businesses, TV and radio sources in Israel. See Figure 2.27.

**Figure 2.27** Home page of the Israel Science and Technology website

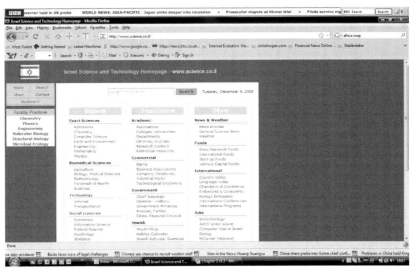

## The United Arab Emirates

Abu Dhabi, the capital of the United Arab Emirates, is the seat of government for the region. Its business and religion interests are male dominated. The city is modern and worthy of description for its architectural structures and modern infrastructure, and it thrives in the internet age. Its former materialistic society is now more aware.

Mention Abu Dhabi and everyone thinks of oil, but oil is not Abu Dhabi's only main interest. The city is an investment hub for infrastructure development, aerospace investment, many types of financial products and global real estate investment. Islamic financing, although not contained just within the UAE or Middle Eastern countries, provides investment funds under the Sharia banking laws.

The best way to delve into Sharia financing is to access the free publications provided by many of the top global law firms that provide and specialise in this area of legal advice. There are also a number of publications from ISI Emerging Markets, Business Islamica and New Horizon.

### New Horizon: *http://www.newhorizon-islamicbanking.com/*

New Horizon is based in London. Some access to the website requires payment, but there's also free content in the form of a quarterly publication, news, hyperlinks to Sharia banking institutions, a glossary and other useful features. See Figure 2.28.

Since the global economic downturn, the Emirates has become a source of funding for international banks.

**Figure 2.28** Home page of the New Horizon website

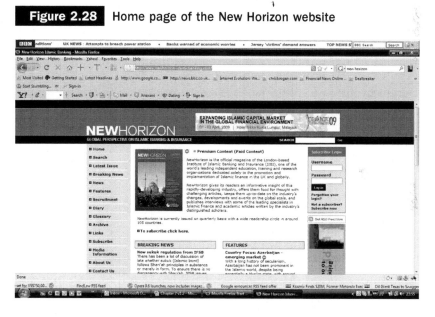

### UAE Business Directory: *http://www.uaebusinessdirectory.com/*

The UAE Business Directory website provides regional news, stock market prices, a link to the Dubai Stock Exchange, and a range of links to education, industries and markets. There are many business-to-business portals for Dubai. See Figure 2.29.

### AskZad: *http://www.askzad.com/English/*

AskZad is a fee-paying service for Middle East data. It offers Arabic-to-English translation services, and claims to be the first and largest Arabic

**Figure 2.29**   Home page of the UAE Business Directory website

digital library with an English interface access to its data. Offerings include news reports, scientific papers, conference materials, dictionaries, Who's Who bibliographies and Arabic books. See Figure 2.30.

**Figure 2.30**   AskZad home page

## Foreign Direct Investment magazine: *http://www.fdimagazine.com/*

*Foreign Direct Investment* (FDI) magazine puts Dubai at the top of its poll on Middle East cities of the future (Figure 2.31).[6]

**Figure 2.31** Results of a poll on the FDI magazine website

# India

India has held out well against the economic downturn so far, and its businesses are growing. Companies globally are vying with each other to do business in India with Indian companies and state-owned entities. Its librarians and information professionals are moving over to electronic content and acknowledge that they are working in exciting electronic-pioneering times as new technology rushes in to assist them in their work. New Delhi is currently undergoing some serious infrastructure upgrades, including a new metro.

There's no lack of access to business information here. The newspapers are accessible online, as are business portals and government websites.

### The Securities and Exchange Board of India: *http://www.sebi.gov.in/*

The Securities and Exchange Board of India (SEBI) website provides clear data on financial regulation in its securities markets. There is also access to an RSS feed so users can bring in updated exchange data regularly. See Figure 2.32.

**Figure 2.32** Home page of the Securities and Exchange Board of India website

## India in Business: *http://www.indiainbusiness.nic.in/*

The India in Business website is another rich source of information. Here you can explore the Indian states, and access monthly economic statistics and various studies and surveys. See Figure 2.33.

**Figure 2.33** Home page of the India in Business website

Indiainfo.com (*http://www.indiainfo.com/*) is a social portal, offering all the usual chat, RSS feeds, shopping, entertainment and sporting information, but it also has large amounts of data on industries, business, economy and relevant associations. It allows researchers to search using the Indian search engine India Focus Search.

Business Standard India (*http://www.business-standard.com/india/*) is an English language newspaper that provides information about the country and its people.

## China

China is a huge country enveloping the special administrative regions of Hong Kong, Macau and Taiwan. It has special economic zones for business enterprises, such as in Shenzhen in the south. The terrain is as changeable as the extreme weather systems that dominate the region. The difference in the language between Mandarin and Cantonese is clear to listeners; the written language remains the same for all.

There are many provinces, all of which have local governments in place, so China is a specialist area for researchers. If you wanted to look at land legislation in the country, it would be a huge challenge, and require someone on the ground to back up your research.

Access to legislation is available, but it changes so frequently that you would need to read the local Chinese language newspapers to access new

**Figure 2.34** Home page of the China Law & Practice website

promulgations. Sometimes it takes time for legislation to get into the electronic system of the government, and when it does you may need to be able to use Big5 on the keyboard. Big5 is the Chinese equivalent of Word. The law firms in the region are a good way to source up-to-date legislation. Use law firms such as Mayer Brown JSM (*http://www .mayerbrown.com/mayerbrownjsm/*), Norton Rose (*http://www.nortonrose .com/*) and China Law and Practice (*http://www.chinalawandpractice.com/ Default.aspx*), where you can obtain full-text translations of numerous types of legislation and deal information. See Figure 2.34.

### The Ministry of Commerce of the PRC: *http://english.mofcom .gov.cn/*

The Ministry of Commerce of the PRC website has a lot of information relating to trade, including statistical data, speeches and information about the officials of the Ministry of Foreign Trade and Economic Cooperation. Access is available in seven languages. The statistical import and export data is set out in detailed criteria and is available by province and special administrative region. See Figure 2.35.

### The Shenzhen Stock Exchange: *http://www.szse.cn/main/en/*

The Shenzhen Stock Exchange is one of the main exchanges in China. It has opened up to more transparency in the trades it deals in, while

**Figure 2.35** Home page of the Ministry of Commerce of the PRC website

**Figure 2.36**  Home page of the Shenzhen Stock Exchange website

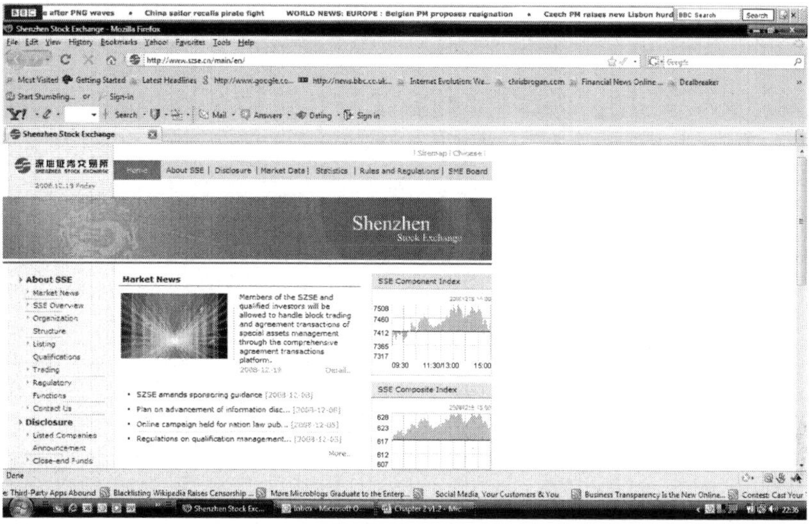

implementing ongoing radical changes to the way it conducts its business. On the website you will locate regulatory data for the Exchange in the areas of listing, market-making, trading, settlement and compliance. See Figure 2.36.

### The China Securities Regulatory Commission: *http://www.csrc .gov.cn/n575458/n4001948/*

The website of the China Securities Regulatory Commission is another valuable source of information. See Figure 2.37.

In January 2009, the press reported that China had become the third largest economy in the world, but take a closer look at from where those statistics were derived. China's National Bureau of Statistics was the source of this news, but it needs to be carefully compared with data from the World Bank and the IMF, which gather their data in a different way, and report their findings differently.

Let's not forget the blogs. The internet is awash with rumours about blogging surveillance, but not all of the blogs originate in China. Victor Shih shares his thoughts on the Chinese political arena at *http:// chinesepolitics.blogspot.com/*.

Asiabizblog (*http://www.asiabizblog.com/archives/2008/12/us_commerce_ dep_1.htm*) is a useful blog for keeping up with new developments in the Asian region. It covers business and law in China and Asia and has been going for seven years. Some of the categories in the blog are Korea,

**Figure 2.37** Home page of the China Securities Regulatory Commission website

Japan, China and Taiwan, banking, intellectual property in Asia and resources and information.

# Hong Kong

Hong Kong is one of China's special administrative regions. Although a part of China, Hong Kong is governed by its own ordinances, which closely reflect English law. Therefore the country has two legislative systems. The ordinances are accessible via the Bilingual Laws Information System (BLIS; *http://www.legislation.gov.hk/eng/home .htm*). See Figure 2.38.

The people in Hong Kong are Cantonese Chinese, friendly, enterprising and quick to spot a business opportunity – they never go anywhere without business cards in their pocket.

The weather systems are as extreme as those in China, matching them closely, and mud slides occur in the heavy rains. There is an incredible weather monitoring system set up via Hong Kong Weather Underground (*http://www.wunderground.com/global/stations/45007.html*), which shows warnings of storms in the shape of coloured clouds on the TV screen.

This beautiful island and its surrounding territory is a financial hub for Asia, and it deals in all types of business from around the world.

**Figure 2.38**  Bilingual Laws Information System home page

## The Hong Kong Exchange: *http://www.hkex.com.hk/index.htm*

The website of the Hong Kong Exchange (HKE) is the place to look for a range of information, from trading arrangements during a typhoon or a black rainstorm to its busy derivatives market. See Figure 2.39.

**Figure 2.39**  Home page of the HKE website

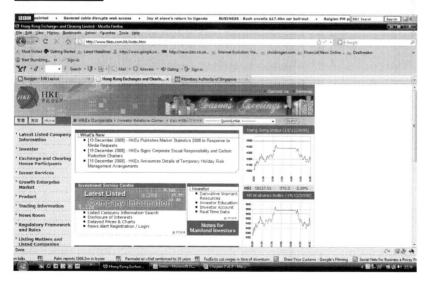

The Hong Kong Trade Development Council (*http://info.hktdc.com/ main/industries/industry.htm*) has profiles and manufacturing statistics of the major industries. There is an overview of the markets, export statistics and industry trends included in each profile.

It is easy to find business and company information in Hong Kong, although if you need unlisted company information you may need to use one of the paid subscription services. The Cyber Search Centre (*http://www.icris.cr.gov.hk/csci/*) of the Integrated Companies Registry Information System is a useful place to start.

## Japan

### Bank of Japan: *http://www.boj.or.jp/en/*

The Bank of Japan publishes many statistical reports that are available in English. There is a lot of financial data on its website that is well worth exploring, to build a picture of the Japanese economy. See Figure 2.40.

English company reports are readily available at a price from publishers such as the *Japan Company Handbook*, published by ToyoKeizai. They are not always cheap to purchase.

**Figure 2.40** Home page of the Bank of Japan website

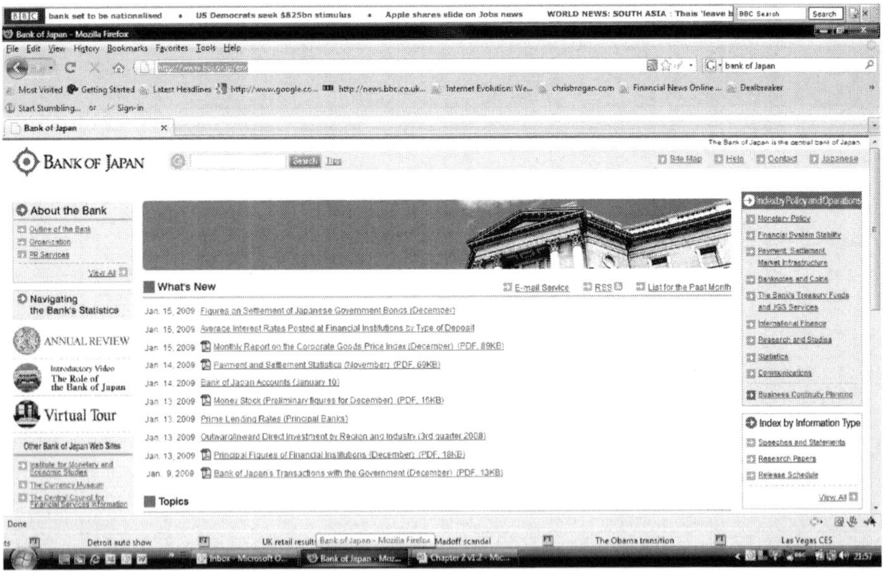

## Japan External Trade Organisation: *http://www.jetro.go.jp/*

The Japan External Trade Organisation (JETRO) website also provides a number of reports and publications in English including a free newsletter on its website. See Figure 2.41.

**Figure 2.41** Home page of the Japan External Trade Organisation website

## Japan Business Information: *http://www.japanbusinessinformation.com/?cat=12*

The Japan Business Information site is a portal for understanding Japanese markets and companies, and has some very useful advice and free resources to point you in the right direction for your research. See Figure 2.42.

## Singapore

On the Southern tip of Malaysia lies Singapore, a country where the humidity and temperature rarely if ever drops below 30° C. Like China and Hong Kong, Singapore has a busy shipping industry.

The business sector of Singapore is relatively easy to locate.

## Contact Singapore Companies: *http://www.contactsingaporecompanies.com/*

The Contact Singapore Companies website provides access to companies operating in Singapore. They are listed by industry sector. See Figure 2.43.

**Figure 2.42** Japan Business Information home page

**Figure 2.43** Home page of Contact Singapore Companies website

**Monetary Authority of Singapore:** *http://www.mas.gov.sg/index.html*

The Monetary Authority of Singapore website is another place to hunt for information. Like all the regulatory bodies, it offers market and statistical data, banking regulations and financial market pricing. See Figure 2.44.

**Figure 2.44** Home page of the Monetary Authority of Singapore website

## Australia and New Zealand

The Australian Government Directory: *http://www.agd.com.au/ directory.php?dirpage=search&act=search&cat=000001&region_id=*

Included in the prolific data about Australia is the Australian Government Directory (AGD), which incorporates Business Australia (Figure 2.45). It has a clean, fast-loading, organised website and it is easy to access information. It isn't hugely populated with data yet, but it's a good start.

### Nationwide Business Directory of Australia: *http://www.nationwide .com.au/*

The Nationwide Business Directory of Australia website is very easy to navigate, intuitive actually, and offers information by territory, general business, franchise services for the indigenous population, government, education and more. See Figure 2.46.

Try a search for financial and investment services in New South Wales and then make a comparison with Tasmania. Do the same again for aircraft services in this massive region. You'll see a picture of extremes and variables.

**Figure 2.45** Home page of the Business Australia website

**Figure 2.46** Home page of the Nationwide Business Directory of Australia website

### The Australian Uranium Association: *http://aua.org.au/*

Have a look at the website of the association for one of Australia's main industries – mining (Figure 2.47). The Australian Uranium Association website is a good source of data for mining uranium. There is a lot of

**Figure 2.47** Home page of the Australian Uranium Association website

information on this site leading to in-depth industry data, publications and research reports, press releases and hyperlinks to related industry bodies.

**IBISWorld:** *http://www.ibisworld.com.au/industry/retail.aspx?indid=69&chid=1&test=2*

You can find industry data from the IBISWorld website on sand mining in Oz, including its industry code, for further searching. You'll only get an overview but you can pay for the rest of the detailed reports available or use the keywords for search enhancement. See Figure 2.48.

Other options are to look at the journals such as *Mining Monthly* or educational resources like Mining Education Australia.

Many Australians like beer and barbeques, and since we were invited to a barbeque, we thought it might be interesting to look at the local beer market. The Little Brewing Company published the results of the Sydney Royal Beer competition to find the best beer. The most interesting section was the list of 'boutique' beers that were made available in the document. See *http://www.thelittlebrewingcompany.com.au/img/Beer_Results_PR.pdf.*

## Figure 2.48　Article on mineral sand mining in Australia on the IBISWorld website

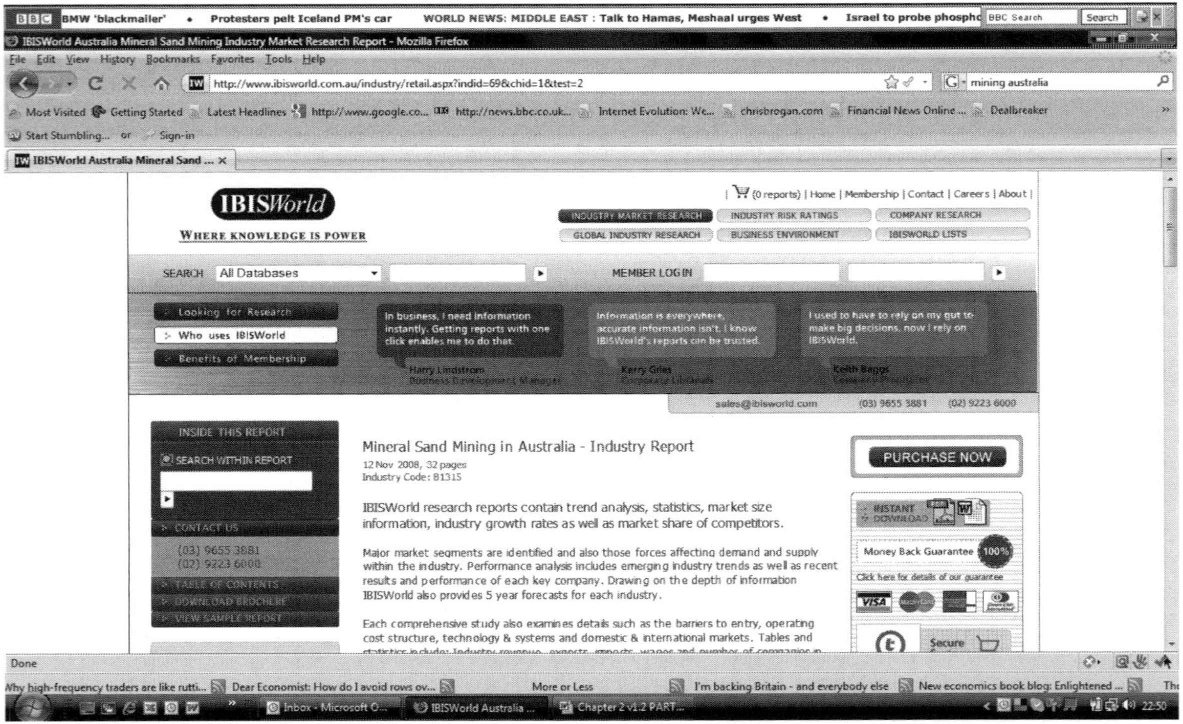

## MarketResearch.com: *http://www.marketresearch.com/ corporate/aboutus/publishers.asp?view=2&*

MarketResearch.com is a commercial research publisher. Registration is required to view the contents pages of the website. It can provide a comprehensive list of publishers of the beverage markets – including beer. See Figures 2.49 and 2.50.

**Figure 2.49** Beer market research reports on the MarketResearch.com website (1)

**Figure 2.50** Beer market research reports on the MarketResearch.com website (2)

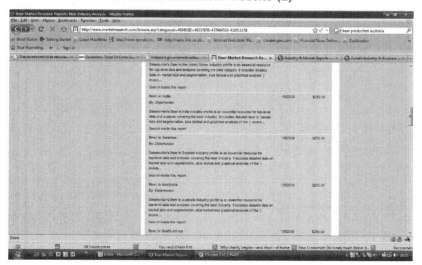

A Euromonitor report at *http://www.euromonitor.com/Beer_in_Australia* allows searchers to view the local players in the Australian beer market, and the Australian Bureau of Statistics (*http://www.abs.gov.au/*) provides data from its website, but researchers may need to deviate to 'hospitality'.

Cuil provided beer data for New Zealand as well as Australia. Clusty returned some good results and the clustering mechanism provided extra results for drilling down further into the data. See Figure 2.51.

**Figure 2.51**  Result of search on Clusty for 'australian beer market'

# The Americas

## Latin America

### RGE Monitor: *http://www.rgemonitor.com/latam-monitor*

I have subscribed to RGE Monitor for a long time. The free stuff, that is. It's invaluable. This regular update is good reading, and provides limited-access global coverage before you pay a subscription fee. The updates are written in plain English and are useful for educational purposes; the economists who write these reports are led by Nouriel Roubini, an eminent economist who was described in the *Wall Street Journal* recently as Dr Doom.[7]

# Figure 2.52 'Latin America EconoMonitor' on RGE Monitor

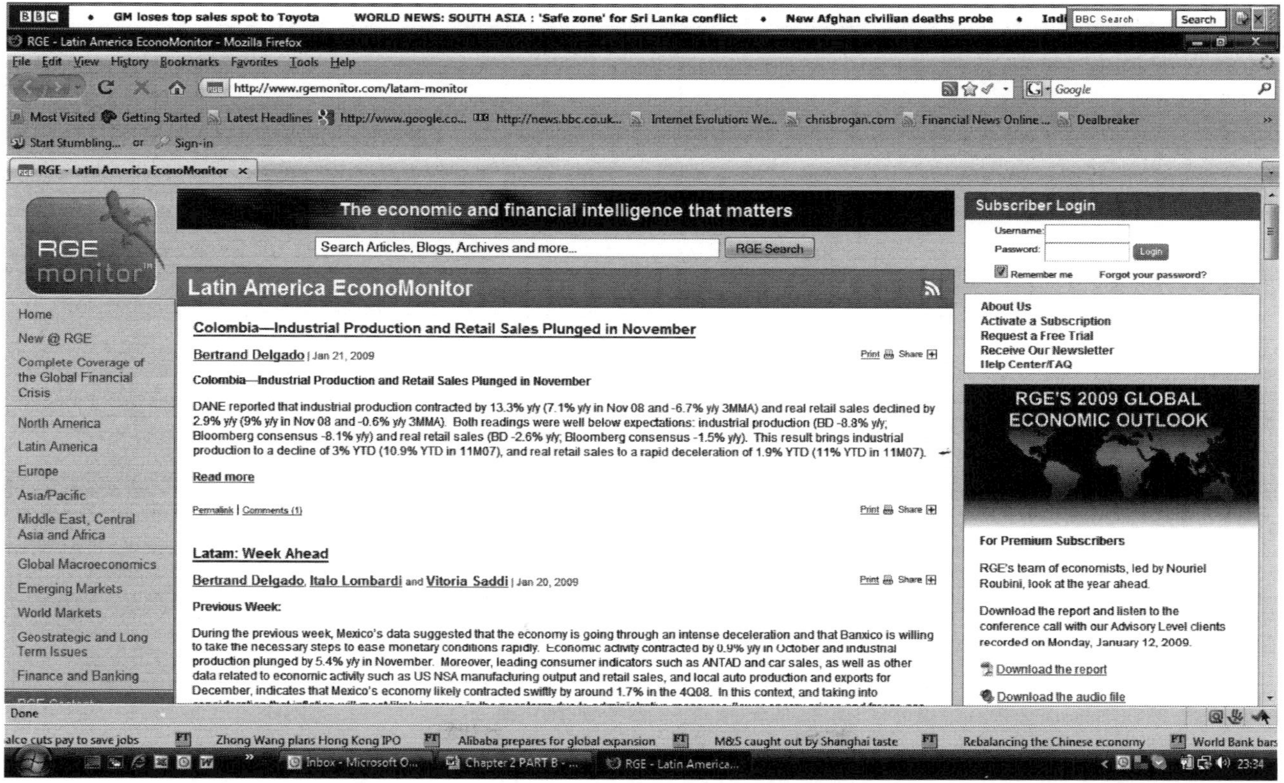

Ignore this website at your loss – that is my personal opinion. It's realistic, not doom mongering. Pay the subscription fee and you have a very rich, varied source of reliable data that is hard to get in one place anywhere else I have looked.

At RGE Monitor you can search Latin America by country and subject. There's a free trial of RGE Monitor content on registration and the site has a number of blogs. See Figure 2.52.

At this point, let's take a look at country ratings. Latin America is an interesting place for this, and there are various ways to make comparisons. Which is your favourite site? Standard & Poor's? Moodys? Fitch? Or how about the Canadian-based DBRS? This contains the DBRS Pari Passu Index (*http://www.dbrs.com/research/226333/pari-passu-index-ye2008 .pdf*), which makes good reading. The main focus is securitisation, structured finance and credit analysis. There's plenty more data in other areas, but you need to register. People want to see who's looking at their data as much as we want to see the data they freely provide to us. That's a fair exchange as long as you know how they may use your data.

## Argentina

Starting in Argentina, we took a closer look at what's on offer in English.

### Onlinenewspapers.com: *http://www.onlinenewspapers.com/*

The newspapers were easy to locate via an Australian website called Onlinenewspapers.com, which provides listings and hyperlinks to global newspapers to make the search easy. See *http://www.onlinenewspapers .com/argentin.htm* for links to newspapers in Argentina (Figure 2.53).

### Ambito.com: *http://www.ambitoweb.com.ar/english/*

Ambito.com, although published in Spanish, has an English edition, where I was able to locate economic data in the financial section, provided by Hernan Hirsch, head of RSH Macroeconomica. The site has hyperlinks to reports from the World Trade Organization, BIS, World Bank, JPMorgan Chase, the Economic Commission for Latin America and the Caribbean (ECLAC), World Economic Forum and IMF, which was useful and reassuring when reliable data may be perceived as hard to come by. See Figure 2.54.

### Energy Information Administration: *http://www.eia.doe.gov/*

Argentina's largest industries are oil and gas and the precious metals sector. The Energy Information Administration, a US government

**Figure 2.53** Links to newspapers in Argentina on Onlinenewspapers.com

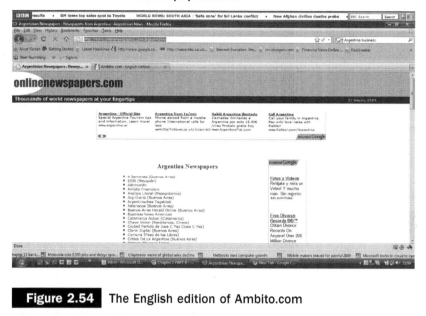

**Figure 2.54** The English edition of Ambito.com

organisation, offers detailed energy consumption data covering global country analysis, including Latin American countries, on its website. See *http://www.eia.doe.gov/emeu/cabs/Argentina/Background.html* for information on Argentina (Figure 2.55). Be aware that the current data

**Figure 2.55** Information on Argentina on the Energy Information Administration website

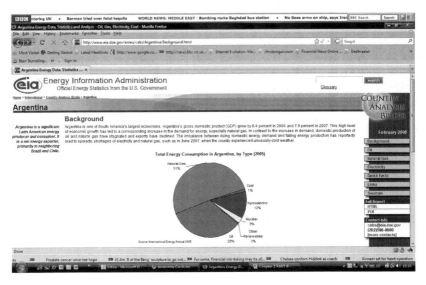

for Argentina only covered up to 2005 in summer 2009. This detailed website covers all types of energy, and has a large variety of historical and other data on market prices and forecasts, geographical overviews and a kids' page for energy projects and learning.

### The Oxford Institute for Energy Studies: *http://www.oxfordenergy .org/links.shtml*

The Oxford Institute for Energy Studies, part of the University of Oxford, has a really good list of global links to related organisations on its website (Figure 2.56). The library services on offer are free or at a heavily discounted price, with the articles provided by top publishing organisations in this sector. There is also access to presentations and seminars.

## *Brazil*

And so we move on to Brazil, a developing country and a developed country intermingled. It has a European feel, a modern underground system, and the Favella community – the poorest people – and street children.

**Figure 2.56** Energy links on the Oxford Institute for Energy Studies website

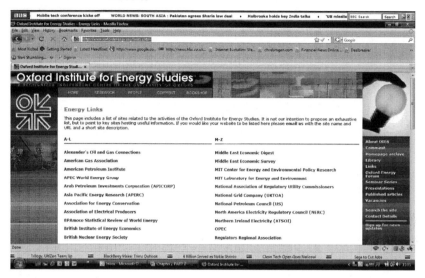

### The International Coffee Organization: http://www.ico.org/index.asp

Brazil is the world's largest producer of coffee. The website of the International Coffee Organization, which is based in London, is a good place to hunt out up-to-date coffee trade and production statistics.

You can read the English version of the Brazilian agency Companhia Nacional de Abastecimento's (CONAB's) final official estimate of the coffee crop for 2009/10. The site has a lot of information about the global coffee industry, including the story of coffee, a coffee vocabulary, statistics, coffee prices, historical data, facts about decaffeination and coffee types, and a list of meetings and events for industry players. See Figure 2.57.

### UNICA Sugar Industry Association: http://english.unica.com.br/apex/

Brazil also produces a large amount of sugar cane as another of its major industries and is diversifying into biofuels. The UNICA Sugar Industry Association is working with APEX Brazil with a view to using ethanol as a renewable source of energy (Figure 2.58). If you were to check the international news against the information on its website, you would see that there appear to be some conflicts over the use of extra land to grow the sugar cane.

**Figure 2.57** Home page of the International Coffee Organization website

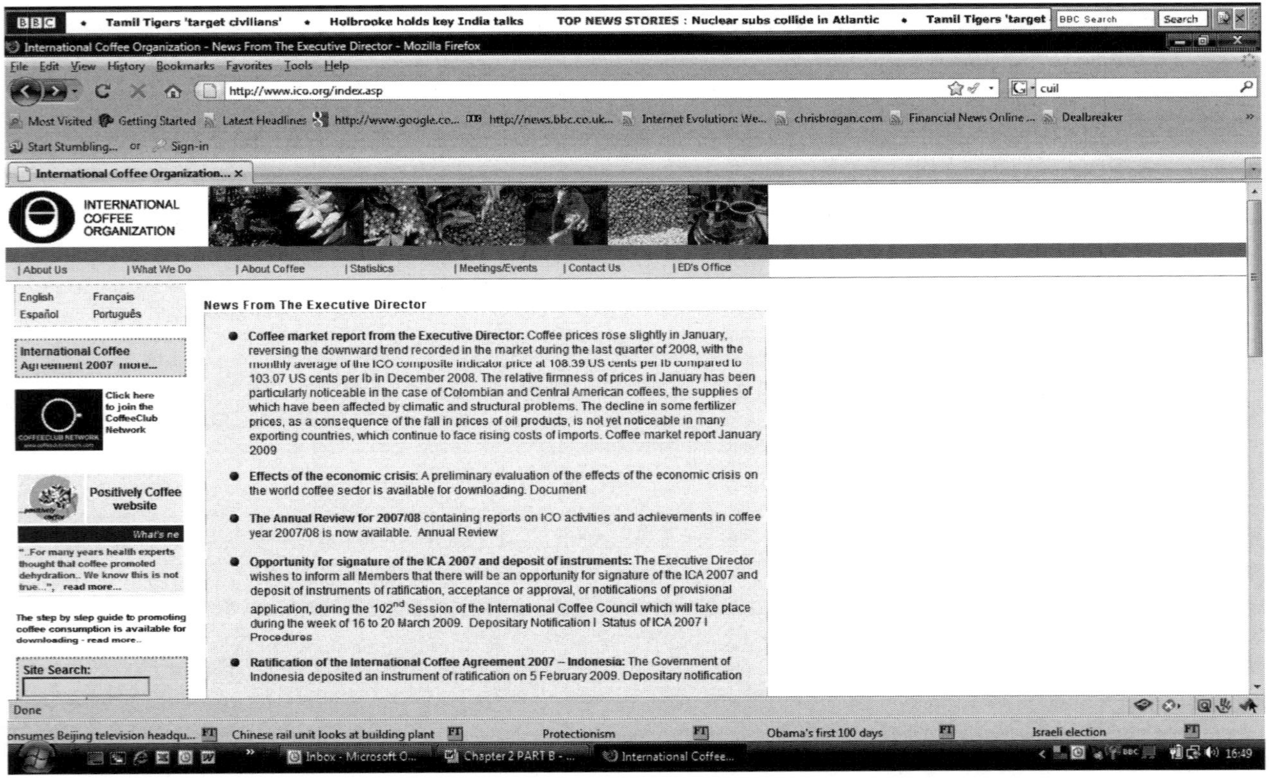

**Figure 2.58** Information about the strategy to promote Brazilian ethanol abroad on the UNICA Sugar Industry Association website

While we're here, we take a look at the (financial) debt markets in Latin America. Brady bonds were thought up in 1989 by Nicholas Brady who was the then US Treasurer. They were a way for international banks to remove developing country debt from their balance sheets before other over-the-counter (OTC) financial instruments like derivatives were invented to become another way of raising off-balance sheet finance.

The Bank for International Settlements (BIS) has a wealth of current data on Brady bonds, and includes historical analysis at *http://www.bis.org/search/?q=brady+bonds&scope=&dr=-1&mp=phrase&_st= false&c=10&sb=1*. See Figure 2.59.

# USA

In the USA everything is larger than life, including the hotel beds, dinners, shopping and playing. Remember that as well as there being different ways for Americans and English people to describe particular items, there are also spelling anomalies and differences in synonyms, acronyms and antonyms; we need to make sure we allow for this disparity between American and UK English as we search.

**Figure 2.59** Result of search on the BIS website for 'Brady bonds'

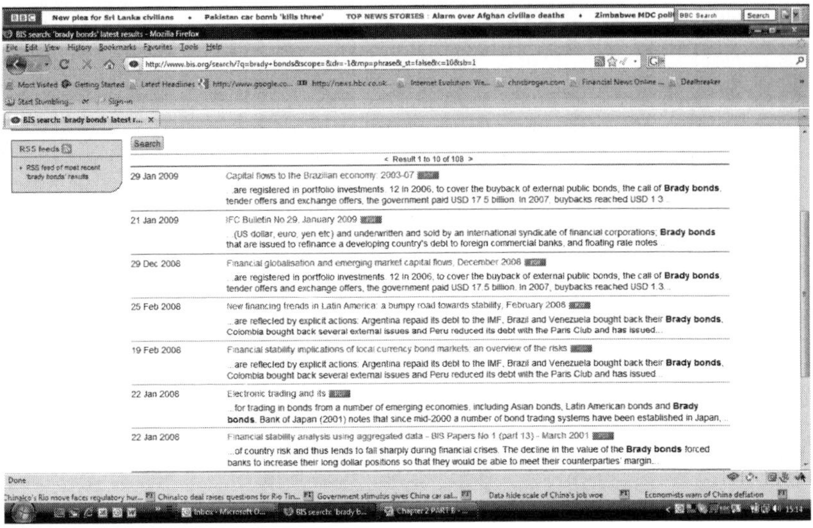

## The Securities and Exchange Commission: *http://www.sec.gov/*

The American regulator, the Securities and Exchange Commission (SEC), has great influence and has taken more offenders down than any other financial regulator at minimal cost and time compared with other regulators. The Division of Trading and Markets website is at *http://www.sec.gov/divisions/marketreg.shtml*. The SEC Regulations (*http://www.sec.gov/about/laws.shtml*) are available from the website and constitute some extremely complicated legislation (Figure 2.60). But one can't complain that it's difficult when it's all sitting there freely available. Get in and look up some of this legislation, for example the Sarbanes-Oxley Act 2002 (*http://www.sec.gov/spotlight/sarbanes-oxley.htm*).

You can also obtain the financial filings of millions of companies using the EDGAR database (*http://www.sec.gov/edgar/quickedgar.htm*), which is available on the SEC website and is a good place to start for company research.

Another interesting area to research is the current status of investment banks. They no longer exist as we knew them – those that are left, such as Goldman Sachs and Morgan Stanley, have changed their banking status and are now regulated by the Federal Reserve Board (*http://www.federalreserve.gov/*) and the Federal Deposit Insurance Corporation (FDIC; *http://www.fdic.gov*).

**Figure 2.60** The laws that govern the securities industry on the SEC website

**The Madoff Ponzi Scheme List of Clients:** *http://image.guardian.co.uk/sys-files/Business/documents/2009/02/05/madoff_list.pdf*

That Madoff Ponzi Scheme List of Clients – how extraordinary! I never would have thought that this document would make it into the public domain, but I am glad to see that it did. What a list! There are so many fingers in so many pies, and just look at the clients where they are represented via a broker. Members of Madoff's own family are also on the list. I wonder how many companies have perused this list to see if any of their current or future business contacts and clients are listed on there. This is a good place to check out the investments of potential new clients, and assist with identifying them, as address and contact details are provided. This huge 163 page document forms part of a court exhibit. See Figure 2.61.

Because Silicon Valley is the USA's hi-tech region, I thought we would take a stroll down there and see what we would find. A basic search came up with a few good results. We found the big names and the big companies and the Silicon Valley website has a few interesting pointers and historical information about the internet pioneers. But another engine took us down another path.

**Figure 2.61** One page of the Madoff Ponzi Scheme List of Clients

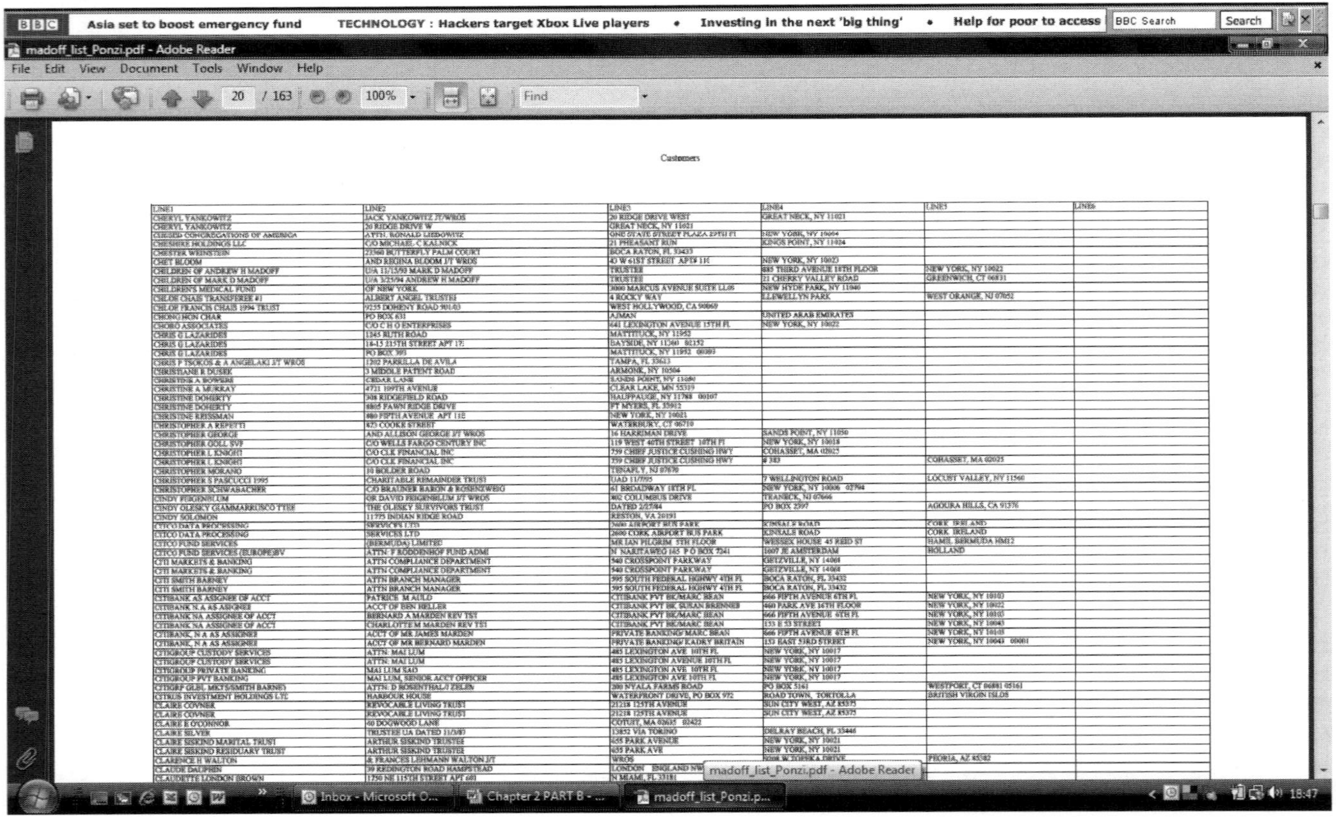

## Techdirt: *http://techdirt.com/*

We found an interesting blog called Techdirt, managed by a company called Floor64 (Figure 2.62). It's a really good blog on the tech industry in the USA and global industry stuff. The topics covered are diverse. I have to call it 'stuff' because you never know what is going to be posted. The day I looked, they were talking about copyright for chess moves... Hello... is anyone on the real planet or just messing on virtual just because they can or because they can make money from it? Virtual chess maybe suddenly gets bought out? How far does this go if every chess move can be copyrighted?

This looks like copyright information gone mad and out of control. Where does copyright end? If our kids have no grandparents or parents who play chess, then is it down to our schools to teach them, and where do their copyright 'rights' lie? Look at the bigger picture. Can legislation take it so far on the net?

Strategy games are an important learning process for all and whether we like it or not they are being introduced into learning centres and libraries. The USA is already pioneering gaming into libraries and in 2009 the American Library Association (*http://www.ala.org/ala/alonline/index.cfm*) covered gaming in an issue of its journal *American Libraries*.

In the UK, I haven't seen any signs of gaming in my locality so far. My own experience of using public libraries for professional research was a

**Figure 2.62**  The Techdirt blog

frustrating one because the firewalls are extreme. I know I could receive a lot of comments for saying this, because the firewalls are there to protect children and copyright, but when I had to look up some research in a public library, I was blocked from accessing what I needed.

## Canada

Further north in Canada the languages spoken are French and English and the Canadian regions consist of provinces and territories. Canada's main industries include wood, pulp and paper, fish and seafood, wheat and mineral extraction.

### Pulp & Paper Canada: *http://www.pulpandpapercanada.com/links/ industryLinks.asp*

Looking at the wood, pulp and paper industries, we went to Pulp&PaperCanada, which has a page of industry links that will allow you to search other organisations covering forestry, industry associations and research centres. See Figures 2.63 and 2.64.

There are links to organisations covering recycled paper, American and UK energy departments, and Pulpandpaper.net, where you can access a list of pulp and paper resources on the internet. There are lots of paths to choose from just on this one site in order to hone your requirements. We located data in both French and English while we searched.

**Figure 2.63** Industry links on the Pulp & Paper Canada website (1)

**Figure 2.64** Industry links on the Pulp & Paper Canada website (2)

The fishing industry is equally interesting with search results providing categorised listings of Canadian government departments, fishing science, commercial fishing and Greenpeace activity measuring the effects of overfishing. Fishingnet.ca (*http://www.fishingnet.ca/ DesktopDefault.aspx*) pointed to an article on NovaNewsNow.com that provided detailed data on Canada's export fish and seafood market for 2008.[8] These details were then broken down by province. The data originated from the rich resource of Fisheries and Oceans Canada (*http://www.dfo-mpo.gc.ca/index-eng.htm*) and the source was quoted appropriately. The copyright policy of the Fisheries and Oceans Canada website and data is stringent, and it is worth researchers taking note of the regulations before using anything from it.

### Canadian Wheat Board: *http://www.cwb.ca/public/en/*

Further on, the website of the Canadian Wheat Board (CWB) provided us with access to data on the wheat industry. The CWB says it is 'the single largest seller of wheat and barley in the world, holding more than 20% of the international market'. On 23 February 2009 it reported on the global crisis and how it has impacted on the price of grain for 2009/10. Covering wheat, durum and feed and designated barley, it provides detailed statistics, commentary and a glossary of the acronyms used to describe each different type of grain. This organisation is controlled by the farmers who market the products. The many different types of grain available always remind me of the different descriptions used for the crude oils on the global commodity exchanges. See Figure 2.65.

**Figure 2.65** The home page of the CWB website

# International organisations

### The Bank for International Settlements: *http://www.bis.org/*

The Bank for International Settlements (BIS) website has some great data for this type of research, which is authoritative and relied on by the financial industry itself. It is constantly used and quoted by them as a source of their data research. There is a wealth of papers available to download. Included on this site is access to regular updates for Basle II legislation, financial stability, systemic risk, regular working papers, derivatives, FX, securities and payment systems. BIS has a list of central banks which also provide free statistical data. See Figure 2.66.

### Securities Industry and Financial Markets Association: *http://www.sifma.org/*

Another good place to look at for information is the website of the Securities Industry and Financial Markets Association (SIFMA) (Figures 2.67 and 2.68). SIFMA is a merger between the Bond Markets Association and the Securities Industry Association. The website

**Figure 2.66** The home page of the BIS website

**Figure 2.67** The home page of the SIFMA website (1)

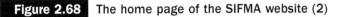

**Figure 2.68** The home page of the SIFMA website (2)

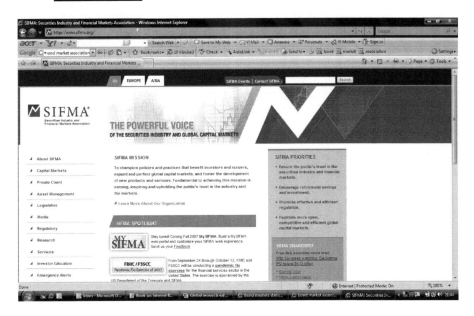

provides access to graphs and statistical data across a broad spectrum, and they can be uploaded to Excel. There is also historical access to data that predates 2000.

Use the tabs at the top of the home page to select access to the US, Europe or Asian markets. Information is available on global capital markets, private client markets, asset management, legislation, regulation and other topics.

### City of London: *http://www.cityoflondon.gov.uk/Corporation/*

The City of London site has a set of research reports available covering financial centres in the EU, Gulf States, India's corporate debt and the Global Financial Centres Index 2008. The reports can be accessed from their publications section (*http://www.cityoflondon.gov.uk/Corporation/ LGNL_Services/Business/Business_support_and_advice/Economic_infor mation_and_analysis/Research_publications/*). See Figure 2.69.

Other excellent sources of information are:

- the Board of Governors of the Federal Reserve (*http://www .federalreserve.gov/econresdata/default.htm*)

- the International Monetary Fund (IMF; *http://www.imf.org/external/ pubind.htm*)

- the Organisation for Co-operation and Development (OECD; *http://www.oecd.org/topic/0,3373,en_2649_34247_1_1_1_1_37467,00 .html*)

- the World Bank (*http://econ.worldbank.org/WBSITE/EXTERNAL/ EXTDEC/0,,menuPK:476823~pagePK:64165236~piPK:64165141~ theSitePK:469372,00.html*)

- the World Trade Organization (WTO; *http://www.wto.org/english/ forums_e/ngo_e/ngosin_e.htm*).

**Figure 2.69**   The City of London website

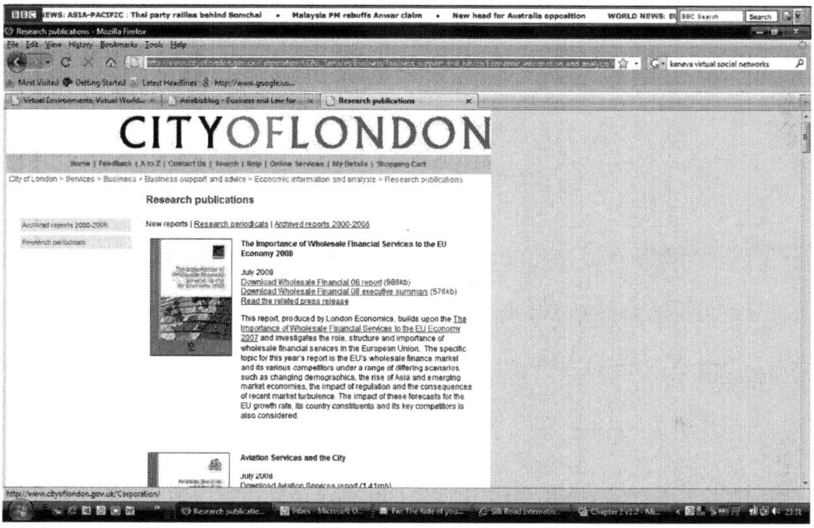

Use these organisations to expand your search strategy by looking through the content on their websites. For instance, on the WTO website, the list of non-government organisations can point you to organisations that cover the industry sector in specific countries (Figure 2.70). It includes the World Trade Center, various chambers of commerce, and many other organisations. If you required Canadian pulp and paper data, you would find the Canadian Pulp and Paper Association listed, from where you can make a narrower search for more specific information.

### Doing Business: *http://www.doingbusiness.org/LawLibrary/*

Another place to obtain business legislation is the World Bank's Doing Business database. This free service allows researchers to compile customised reports. See Figure 2.71.

**Figure 2.70** A list of NGOs on the WTO website

**Figure 2.71** The Law Library page on the Doing Business website

And so we have arrived at the end of this particular journey and hope that you have enjoyed your time and learned something new. It's your turn to go travelling and discover new places, people, legislation and industries. Whatever the question, you can locate a reliable and informed answer.

# List of websites mentioned in this chapter

African Studies Centre (University of Pennyslvania) *http://www.africa
.upenn.edu/asc/bussguide.html*
AgroWeb Russian Federation *http://www.cnshb.ru/awl.%5Cshow
.asp?page=sci\iv*
AllMyFaves *http://www.allmyfaves.com/*
Ambitoweb.com *http://www.ambitoweb.com.ar/english/*
American Library Association *http://www.ala.org/ala/alonline/index.cfm*
Anonymouse *http://anonymouse.org/cgi-bin/anon-www.cgi/*
Asiabizblog *http://www.asiabizblog.com*
AskZad *http://www.askzad.com/English/*
Australian Bureau of Statistics *http://www.abs.gov.au/*
Australian Government Directory *http://www.agd.com.au/directory
.php?dirpage=search&act=search&cat=000001&region_id=*
Australian Uranium Association *http://aua.org.au/*
Bank for International Settlements *http://www.bis.org/*
Bank of Japan *http://www.boj.or.jp/en/*
Bilingual Laws Information System (BLIS) *http://www.legislation.gov
.hk/eng/home.htm*
Business Standard India *http://www.business-standard.com/india/*
Canadian Wheat Board *http://www.cwb.ca/public/en/*
China Law and Practice *http://www.chinalawandpractice.com/Default
.aspx*
China Securities Regulatory Commission *http://www.csrc.gov.cn/n575458/
n4001948/*
Chinese Politics Blog *http://chinesepolitics.blogspot.com/*
CIA World Factbook *https://www.cia.gov/cia/publications/factbook/*
City of London *http://www.cityoflondon.gov.uk*
CoinMill *http://coinmill.com/*
Contact Singapore Companies *http://www.contactsingaporecompanies
.com/*
Craigslist *http://www.craigslist.org/about/*
Cuil *http://www.cuil.com*
Cyber Search Centre *http://www.icris.cr.gov.hk/csci/*
DBRS *http://www.dbrs.com/research/226333/pari-passu-index-ye2008
.pdf*
Dewey & LeBouef *http://www.russianlaws.com/resources/*
Economist Intelligence Unit *http://www.eiu.com*
Energy Information Administration *http://www.eia.doe.gov/emeu/cabs/
Argentina/Background.html*

Euromonitor *http://www.euromonitor.com/beer_in_Australia*
Europa *http://europa.eu/*
European Association of Directory and Database Publishers *http:// www.eadp.org/index.php?q=DIRECTORIES*
Fear and Loathing in Financial Products Blog *http://www.wilmott .com/blogs/satyajitdas/index.cfm/2009/4/12/Credit-Default-Swaps— Through-The-Looking-Glass*
Federal Reserve *http://www.federalreserve.gov/*
Fishingnet.ca *http://www.fishingnet.ca*
Foreign Direct Investment Magazine *http://www.fdimagazine.com*
Google Earth *http://earth.google.com/intl/en_uk/userguide/v4/#fivethings*
Hong Kong Exchange *http://www.hkex.com.hk/index.htm*
Hong Kong Trade Development Council *http://info.hktdc.com/main/ industries/industry.htm*
Hong Kong Weather Underground *http://www.wunderground.com/global/ stations/45007.html*
IBISWorld *http://www.ibisworld.com.au*
IMF *http://www.imf.org*
Index Mundi *http://www.indexmundi.com/world/demographics_profile .html*
India in Business *http://www.indiainbusiness.nic.in/*
Indiainfo *http://www.indiainfo.com/*
International Coffee Organization *http://www.ico.org/index.asp*
International Institute of Social History *http://www.iisg.nl/abb/*
Internet Evolution *http://www.internetevolution.com/*
Intute *http://www.intute.ac.uk/*
Israel Science and Technology *http://www.science.co.il/*
Japan Business Information *http://www.japanbusinessinformation.com/ ?cat=12*
Japan External Trade Organisation *http://www.jetro.go.jp/*
Library of Congress *http://www.loc.gov/rr/international/amed/southafrica/ resources/southafrica-search.html*
Little Brewing Company *http://www.thelittlebrewingcompany.com.au/ img/Beer_Results_PR.pdf*
MarketResearch.com *http://www.marketresearch.com/corporate/aboutus/ publishers.asp?view=2&*
Mashada.com *http://www.mashada.com*
Mayer Brown JSM *http://www.mayerbrown.com/mayerbrownjsm/*
MBendi *http://mbendi.co.za/index.htm*
Ministry of Commerce PRC *http://english.mofcom.gov.cn/*
Monetary Authority of Singapore *http://www.mas.gov.sg/index.html*

Nairobi Stock Exchange *http://www.nse.co.ke/newsite/index.asp*
Nationwide Business Directory of Australia *http://www.nationwide
.com.au/*
New Horizon *http://www.newhorizon-islamicbanking.com/*
Norton Rose *http://www.nortonrose.com/*
NovaNewsNow.com *http://www.novanewsnow.com/article-313731-
Minister-announces-2008-export-figures-for-Canadas-fish-and-
seafood-products.html*
Oanda *http://www.oanda.com/*
OECD *http://www.oecd.org*
Onlinenewspapers.com *http://www.onlinenewspapers.com/*
Open Directory Project (DMOZ) *http://www.dmoz.org/*
Oxford Institute for Energy Studies *http://www.oxfordenergy.org/
links.shtml*
PricewaterhouseCoopers *http://www.pwc.com/*
Privacy International *http://www.privacyinternational.org/*
Pulp & Paper Canada.com *http://www.pulpandpapercanada.com*
Pulpandpaper.net *http://www.pulpandpaper.net/*
RGE Monitor *http://www.rgemonitor.com/latam-monitor*
Search Engine Colossus *http://www.searchenginecolossus.com/*
Securities and Exchange Board of India *http://www.sebi.gov.in/*
Securities and Exchange Commission *http://www.sec.gov/*
Shenzhen Stock Exchange *http://www.szse.cn/main/en/*
SIFMA *http://www.sifma.org/*
Silobreaker *http://www.silobreaker.com/*
Statistics Sweden *http://www.ssd.scb.se/databaser/makro/start
.asp?lang=2*
Superdirectories *http://www.superdirectories.com/?Branch_ID=551319*
Techdirt *http://techdirt.com/*
Tourismtrade.org *http://www.tourismtrade.org.uk*;
now VisitBritain.org (see below)
UAE Business Directory *http://www.uaebusinessdirectory.com/*
UNICA Sugar Industry Association *http://english.unica.com.br/apex/*
VisitBritain.org *http://www.visitbritain.org/*
World Bank *http://econ.worldbank.org/*
World Bank Doing Business Guides *http://www.doingbusiness.org/
LawLibrary/*
World Trade Organization *http://www.wto.org/english/forums_e/ngo_e/
ngosin_e.htm*
Xrates.com *http://www.x-rates.com/cgi-bin/hlookup.cgi*

# Notes

1. Richard Waters, Robin Kwong and Robin Harding, 'Google still struggling to conquer outposts', *Financial Times*, 16 September 2008, at *http://us.ft .com/ftgateway/superpage.ft?news_id=fto0916200812274007266&page=2*.
2. Bryan Burrough, *Barbarians at the Gate: The Fall of RJR Nabisco* (London: Cape, 1990); Philippe Jorion, *Big Bets Gone Bad: Derivatives and Bankruptcy in Orange County* (San Diego: Academic Press, 1995); Mark Pollock and Ross Whitaker, *Making it Happen* (Cork: Mercier Press, 2005); Charles Raw, *Slater Walker: An Investigation of a Financial Phenomenon* (London: Deutsch, 1977) and Nick Leeson, *Rogue Trader* (London: Little, Brown, 1966).
3. Satyajit Das, 'Credit default swaps – through the looking glass', 12 April 2009, at *http://www.wilmott.com/blogs/satyajitdas/index.cfm/2009/4/12/ Credit-Default-Swaps—Through-The-Looking-Glass*.
4. Eduard L. Akim, 'Russian pulp and paper industry in 2007-2008', at *http://www.fao.org/forestry/media/15232/1/0/*.
5. Stephen Saunders, *Rwanda's Internet Evolution*, video, at *http://www .internetevolution.com/document.asp?doc_id=168518)*.
6. Charles Piggott, 'Middle East cities & special economic zones of the future 2008/09', *Foreign Direct Investment Magazine*, 17 December 2008, at *http://www.fdimagazine.com/news/fullstory.php/aid/2635/Middle_East_ Cities___Special__Economic_Zones__of_the_Future_2008_09.html*.
7. Tunku Varadarajan, '"Nationalize" the banks: Dr Doom says a takeover and resale is the market-friendly solution', *Wall Street Journal*, 22 February 2009, at *http://online.wsj.com/article/SB123517380343437079.html*.
8. NovaNewsNow.com, 'Minister announces 2008 export figures for Canada's fish and seafood products', at *http://www.novanewsnow.com/article-313731- Minister-announces-2008-export-figures-for-Canadas-fish-and-seafood- products.html*.

# 3

# Do you know your customer?

Whether you are checking a company before taking out a subscription, looking for a particular person, looking for any litigation on a company that could affect a new business venture or keeping yourself and your organisation safe from internet predators, you need to do your research.

We have already looked at how to identify reliable information in the form of websites, portals, gateways and so on, and the use of that information. Let's now look at how we interact or react to information we haven't asked to receive. Who are we dealing with? How do we identify them and how do we keep ahead of the many internet scams that constantly bombard us via our e-mail systems?

When we are tourists we are often at the mercy of scammers and fraudsters, with no opportunity to check who we are dealing with. We will pay through the nose for goods that are available to the locals at a fraction of the price if we don't know the region or country well, or do not barter or challenge the deal. When you are travelling the world with your mouse, however, there's no excuse for not checking who you are dealing with. Together you will be able to locate information before you part with your cash or provide services or hire someone else's services.

## Dodgy activities on the internet

The internet is a bustling network of activity that is prime estate for fraud, scams, phishing, pharming, bugs, viruses, trojans, worms and many other dodgy activities. Has anyone used your e-mail address to send out bulk e-mail across the world? If this has happened to you, then you know the problems involved when you start a new e-mail address and change over all your contacts to it. There are no boundaries for the sender to send or for the potential victim to be the recipient of abuse. And the problem is that once defended, the writers of these nasty programs continue to develop ever more sophisticated methods to catch us out. As I write, there are new attacks being developed to find us and infiltrate our personal information.

The traffic that drops through the inbox of your e-mail system doesn't automatically end up being fed to the spam folder. If opened, it can be highly damaging to your computer and files, infecting your hardware and applications and incapacitating your mouse.

Among the spam for medical and other aids, drugs, sex and other predators looking to access your personal data, there are scammers attempting to access your money via your bank accounts. Some of it is very obvious and easily avoided, but some is very cleverly assembled. Secure systems are being infiltrated to trap the unwary. PayPal, for instance, has installed a defence mechanism, and always includes a message on its correspondence to customers to allow it to be identified as genuine e-mail from them before it is opened. You need to use the viewing panel in your e-mail system to identify the message as genuine before touching it.

## Preventing internet fraud

### FraudWatch International: *http://www.fraudwatchinternational.com*

FraudWatch International is a commercial internet security site that specialises in phishing activities and offers products that give protection. It is a valuable place to monitor phishing activities because it offers a free newsletter and phishing alerts for the latest scams, which are also available via RSS feeds. There is a facility to allow users to report new scams. The service is global, and offers global information on identity theft, internet fraud, lottery scams and Nigerian 419 scams. See Figures 3.1 and 3.2.

In the section on fraud, FraudWatch International offers more advice about what spam is and how to avoid it.

### National Consumers' League for Internet Fraud: *http://www.fraud.org/internet/inttip/inttip.htm.*

There are thousands of newsletters that you can subscribe to that will keep you up to date with new potential threat developments on the internet. The National Consumers' League for Internet Fraud is a UK organisation offering information on different types of internet fraud. See Figure 3.3.

# Figure 3.1 FraudWatch International home page

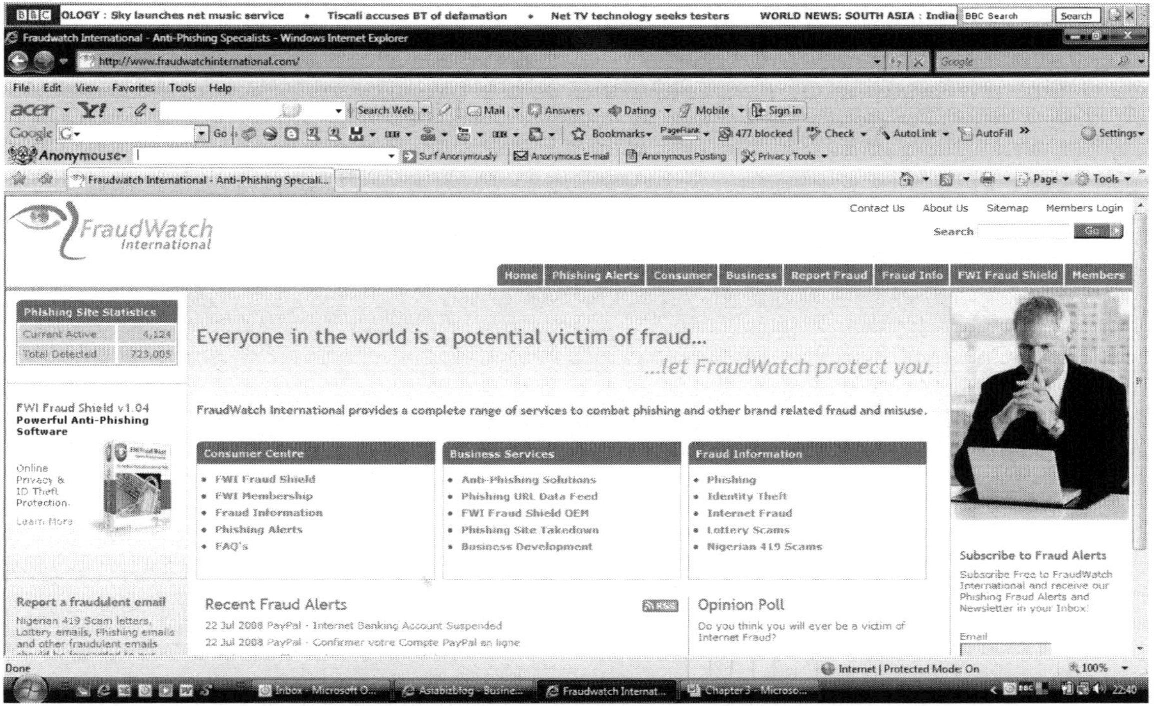

**Figure 3.2**    A fake website shown on FraudWatch International

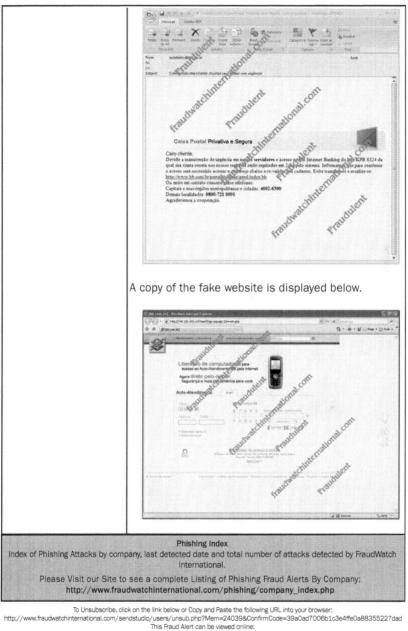

A copy of the fake website is displayed below.

**Phishing Index**
Index of Phishing Attacks by company, last detected date and total number of attacks detected by FraudWatch International.

Please Visit our Site to see a complete Listing of Phishing Fraud Alerts By Company:
**http://www.fraudwatchinternational.com/phishing/company_index.php**

**Figure 3.3** Internet fraud tips listed on the National Consumers' League for Internet Fraud website

The FBI, SEC, Trading Standards Board and most other public government websites offer information about avoiding getting caught by predators. And don't forget the blogs, lists and forums! Use those local to your country, region or area of interest, and then expand the search for a more global idea of what is happening, who the targets are and what the infiltrators are attempting to obtain. See the article 'How to avoid the 10 worst internet scams in 2008' (Figure 3.4).[1]

### DMOZ: *http://www.dmoz.org/Society/Issues/Fraud/Internet/*

DMOZ, The Open Directory Project, has a list of topics about internet fraud. See Figure 3.5.

The banks that are sometimes being used as the conduit for the scam also take a defensive stance, by providing information to their clients who bank with them. JPMorgan Chase posted a report about their customers who were being targeted and suggested ways to identify fraudulent communications (Figure 3.6).[2] It includes contact details, as do all the other financial institutions, so that suspicious e-mails can be reported to them.

**Figure 3.4**  The article 'How to avoid the 10 worst internet scams in 2008' on the Cybercases blogspot

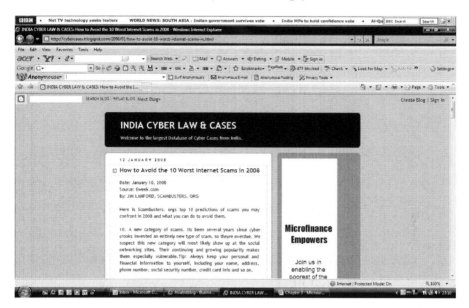

**Figure 3.5**  Search page on DMOZ

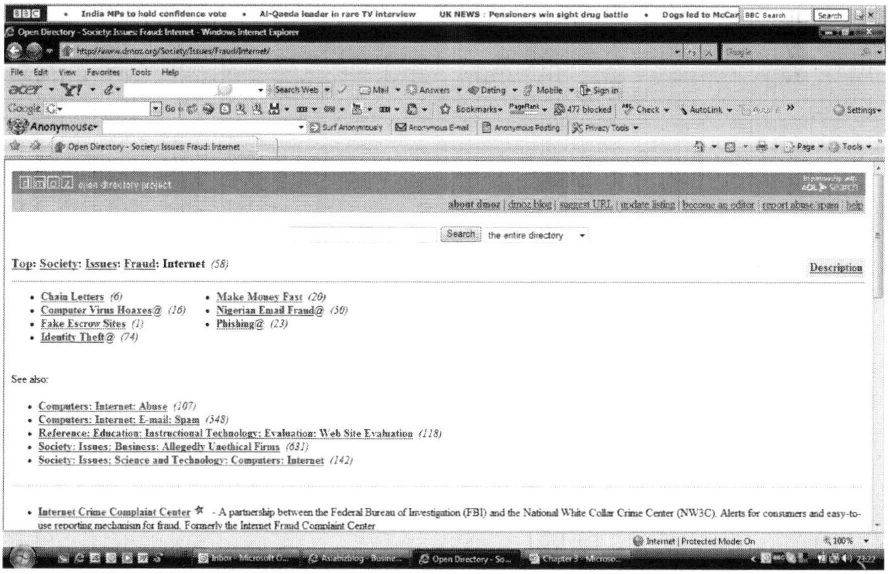

### Figure 3.6 Information on internet fraud and identity theft on the JPMorgan Chase website

The finance industry is required by various legislation and regulations to undertake proper due diligence checks before conducting business with a client. There are no particular cross-border standards being followed at this time, but the relevant agencies involved in this work provide guidelines to encourage standard practices. Each institution is governed not only by jurisdictional legislation and rules, but also by their own ethical standards. Financial institutions use rigorous in-house applications and databases to follow their transactions, to enable them to report any suspicious activity by a client that could be related to money laundering or terrorist activities and work with the Financial Action Task Force on Money Laundering (FATF).

### Financial Action Task Force: *http://www.fatf-gafi.org/pages/ 0,3417,en_32250379_32235720_1_1_1_1_1,00.html*

The Financial Action Task Force has produced a blacklist of countries that would not co-operate with FATF's 40+9 recommended guidelines (Figure 3.7). These countries were known as non-cooperative territories or countries. By October 2006, all nations were co-operating with FATF guidelines and the list was emptied. You can see the history of this work from the FATF web pages on the website. FATF collaborates with other agencies such the OECD, G7, IMF and the BIS.

**Figure 3.7** List of non-cooperative countries and territories on the FATF website

Bank for International Settlements: *http://www.bis.org/*

The Bank for International Settlements (BIS) provides a lot of global information written by the world's central banking bodies and leaders. Subjects covered include transparency, money laundering, terrorist

**Figure 3.8** Result of a search on the BIS website for 'fatf'

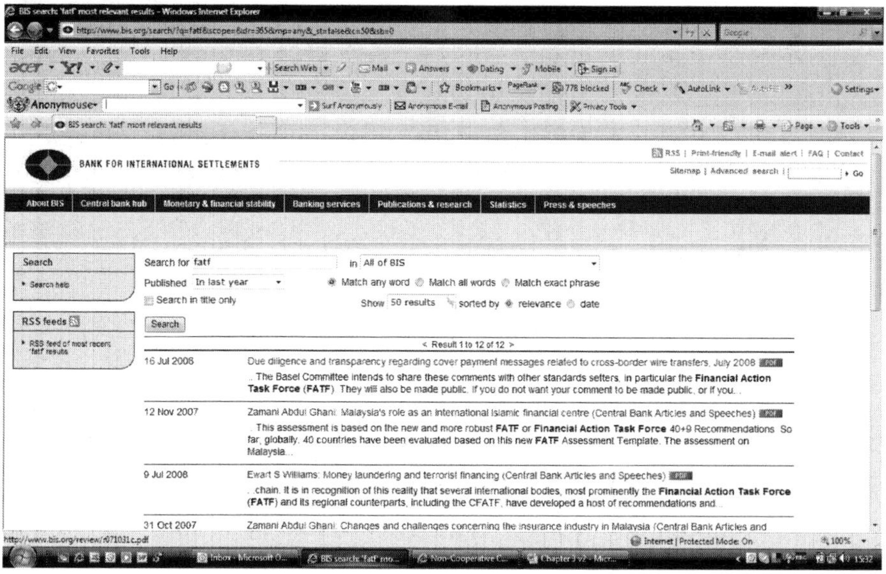

financing, Islamist states and financing, and other issues related to cross-border electronic transfers of money. See *http://www.bis.org/search/?q=fatf&scope=&dr=365&mp=any&_st=false&c=50&sb=0* (Figure 3.8).

## Investment banks

To get a feel for how the investment banks structure their operations, take a look through their websites.

### Goldman Sachs: *http://www2.goldmansachs.com/*

Goldman Sachs explains how its legal and compliance departments are structured and the types of professionals they employ to undertake this important work (Figure 3.9). The legal and compliance teams work with many different departments and interact with each other globally to produce a rigorous safety net for catching illegal activities. This work includes monitoring their own employees' trading activities and providing regular training to ensure that each employee is aware of their professional responsibilities and obligations to the organisation.

**Figure 3.9** Information about global compliance on the Goldman Sachs website

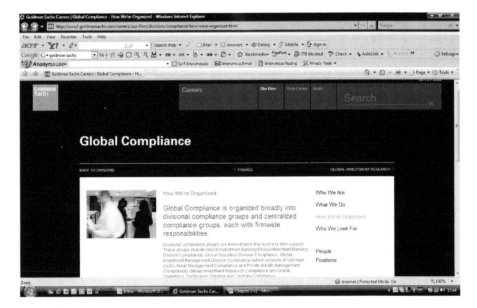

# Ensuring that customer data is secure

An article in *Information Age* by Pete Swabey explains how we are giving away valuable information and data, without even knowing it (Figure 3.10).[3] Swabey said that Britain's Information Commissioner commented in strong terms about the security breaches where customer data had been 'exposed to the public – and possibly criminal gaze'. Internet security company McAfee surveyed 1,400 organisations and came up with data that demonstrated that only 6 per cent of the respondents could categorically state they had not experienced any data loss in the last two years.

The article continues with insights into the risks of insider breaches by employees who leak data externally. Later it discusses the growing problem of employees removing internal data using mass storage devices, in order to sell on the data. Motivated by money, politics or beliefs, it is a growing concern. Swabey highlighted the growing importance of making stringent background checks on employees, as it appears that some employees already hold criminal convictions for these types of offences.

So, on this subject, we consider the hiring of new employees. An organisation needs to know whom they are inviting to join them. What is required is a very thorough background check before an offer of

**Figure 3.10** Article by Pete Swabey on the Information Age website

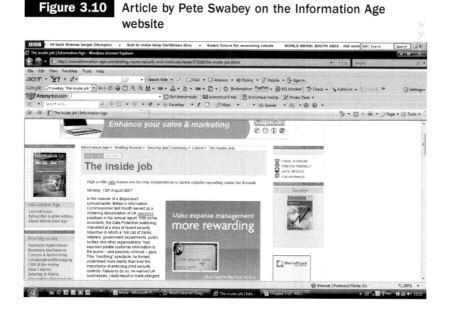

employment drops through the electronic letterbox. There are many companies who undertake this work – for a fee – and later in this chapter some ways are set out for checking people without using an agency.

### Kroll: *http://www.kroll.com/services/screening/krs/*

One of the many agencies undertaking this work on behalf of large organisations is a company called Kroll, whose many services in the investigation industry cover North America, Latin America, the Caribbean, Europe, the Middle East, Africa and Asia. See Figure 3.11.

### Corporate Investigations India: *http://www.corporateinvestigationsindia.com/*

Regionally, there are companies providing country-specific employee background checks. Corporate Investigations India specialises in India, Nepal, Sri Lanka and Bangladesh. See Figure 3.12.

### ESR: *http://www.esrcheck.com/international.php*

The American company ESR also provides global employee screening. See Figure 3.13.

**Figure 3.11**    The Employment Reference Database on the Kroll website

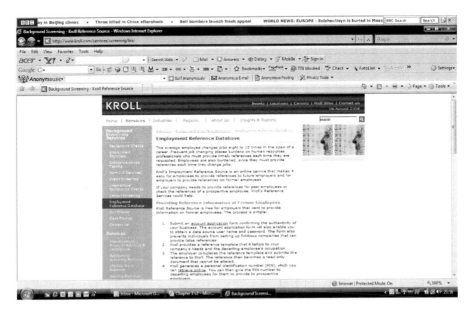

**Figure 3.12** The home page of the Corporate Investigations India website

**Figure 3.13** Information about international screening on the ESR website

**Awareness Watch™ Newsletter:** *http://www.awarenesswatch.com/*
Know your client is such a fascinating subject that it is possible to get so deep into it that you don't surface for hours! Marcus P. Zillman produces a free newsletter called Awareness Watch™ Newsletter (Figure 3.14). He covers an incredible number of topics, and wrote a report in May 2008 on privacy and security resources and sites. His newsletter is well written and provides lists of reliable resources on many topics. He writes a blog, has written numerous books and is also a trainer.

**Figure 3.14** Awareness Watch™ Newsletter

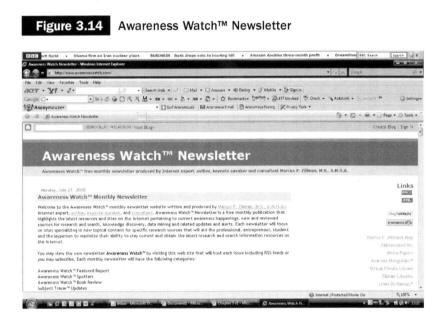

# With whom are you dealing?

On your travels you met someone at a business function and talked at length about a possible venture. Business cards were exchanged, and you agreed to make further contact. Before even thinking about a potential business venture, look at what is on the card you were given. Name, position, contact details, e-mail address, company name, website, description of the company business interests.

All this information is useful. You want to identify the company, the people and whether it is the type of organisation you would want to do business with. This is where the fun starts, as there's an element of dirt-digging. You are looking for any reason why you might want to turn down this new opportunity and more reasons why you should proceed with it. It is your company and/or your reputation that is at risk if you fail to identify a potential new venture partner, customer, client or employee properly. Also your industry is probably regulated to ensure that some checks are made in advance of a potential deal.

On one occasion when undertaking this type of work, I left my desk and walked the streets to identify a specific company and their address when there was an anomaly in the data gathered. My instincts were correct; their offices were not at the address my contact had given. If it is possible and necessary, make a physical location check, so the organisation is where it says it is, if you suspect something isn't right. Gut reaction can be useful, so don't ignore it.

## The 'know-your-customer' grid

Prepare a 'know-your-customer' grid and fill in the gaps. Turn it into a standard form and use it if you need to identify anyone or any business, to provide consistency with the research, whether you are interested in a company, industry or individual. Always cover the same questions to obtain results that can be measured and compared. What cannot be located on the internet can be filled in later using a decent proprietary database.

Spend a little time to get the information you need to complete the final pieces of the jigsaw. First, head for the company website and see what's on the home page. Consider the following points:

- Is it the headquarters or a subsidiary of the main company? Where are the office(s) located? How many staff are there?
- Is the corporate structure clear?
- Note the terminology used to describe the business as it will offer industry-standard keywords for searching more accurately.
- Look at the mission statement: what are the company's ethics?
- Where does the company plan to expand in the future? Consider takeovers, new areas of business, financial investment in people, and so on.
- Look at press releases – what is the company proud of? Has it ventured into a new area or does it plan to do so in the near future? With whom? Check out other companies.

- Are there any podcasts available? If so, watch them and make notes.

- Is there a search box provided on the website? If so, enter keywords related to the business and see what type of information is provided for public consumption. Enter document types – .doc, .pdf, .ppt, .xls and so on. Sometimes the unexpected has been loaded into the website waiting to be found by the inquisitive.

- Is it a publicly listed or a private company? If listed, what exchange(s) is it listed on? Share price movements? Before the current turmoil in the global markets, I would see if there was any sharp volatility in share prices, and what may be the cause. However, that's a given now that many companies have lost market share. Note dates and check against news reports and litigation. World-newspapers.com (*http://www.world-newspapers.com/world-news.html*) is a useful place to look (Figure 3.15), or World News Network (*http://www.wn.com/*).

- Look at annual report availability if it is a public company.

- Look for CEOs, directors, heads of finance, and heads of legal, tax and research departments – anyone who is given exposure as a leader. List names and positions. Even with the loss of jobs that we are currently experiencing, corporate websites should be up to date. Research each individual using more than one different search engine,

**Figure 3.15** World-newspapers.com home page

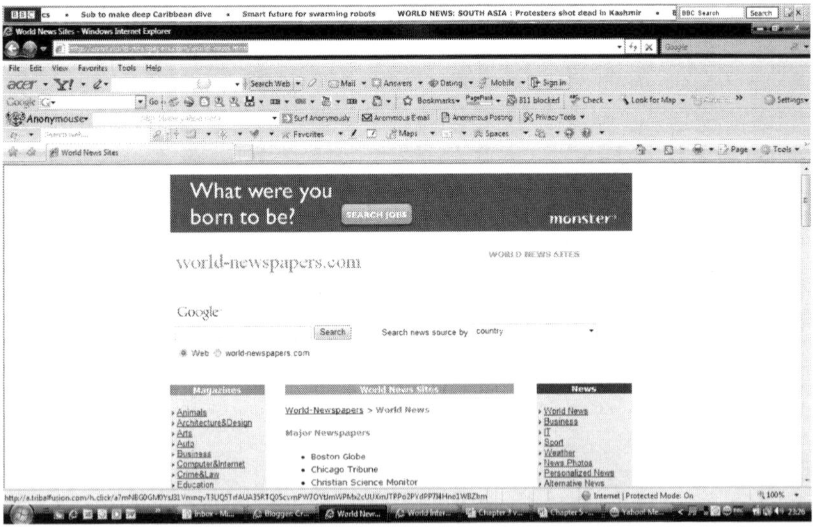

then go to industry gateways and deep web tools, where the data may be sitting behind a log-in screen or in a format that can't be indexed by a spider. Use social networks, podcasts, discussion forums, local newspapers, radio and industry portals. Check conferences for speakers. What did you find? Do these people have unusual outside interests or hobbies? Are they squeaky-clean or Teflon-coated?

- Does the company produce a company magazine? Look for more leaders' names and commentary.

- Go to case law websites such as those for the British and Irish Legal Information Institute (BAILII; *http://www.bailii.org/*) or the World Legal Information Institute (WorldLII; *http://www.worldlii.org/*), which provides multi-jurisdictional case data (Figure 3.16). Search by region for any litigation the company or its subsidiaries have been involved in. How does this affect its projected plans? Has it damaged its reputation in any way? Look for related cases for any precedents that have previously been set.

- Look for pending litigation in the press and City gossip pages, which are available online. For examples of gossip pages and discussion postings, the *South China Morning Post* has 'Lai See', *Private Eye* has 'In the City by City Slicker' and the *Financial Times* has 'The Lex column'. The Lex column posted a request for readers to nominate

**Figure 3.16** The home page of the World Legal Information Institute website

their candidate for the Lex Overpaid CEO award and offered readers the opportunity to air their views about boardroom compensation. What a great way to obtain opinion 'on the ground' and listen to rumours! Make a note and investigate the rumours. There are a number of business rumour sites that can be used to track companies and individuals. Although some rumours may be written by disgruntled employees, others hold enough weight to have a detrimental effect on a company's share price or an individual's reputation. With regard to reputation, keeping a balanced view is important. Assess whether the rumour is spiteful or even slanderous and if it should be ignored. Cyber-bullying does exist. There's a huge amount of personal data out there, and the internet is not always put to the best possible use with the best intentions.

## Business blogs

Nobody's Business (*http://www.theglobeandmail.com/blogs/nobodysbusiness*) is a good example of business blogging, and there are many other good quality blogs that look at those who are less than transparent in their business dealings. See Figure 3.17.

**Figure 3.17** Article by Patricia Best on the Nobody's Business website

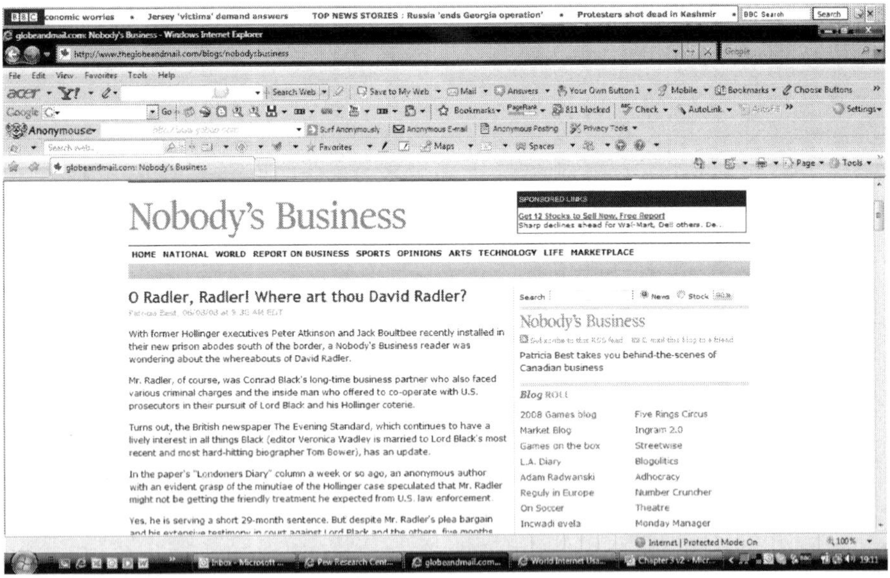

There's a blog on BoingBoing (*http://www.boingboing.net/2008/08/12/ walmart-you-cant-sca.html#comment-258345*) about use of the photocopying services offered in WalMart, the copying of historical photos of relatives from a hundred years ago, and the copyright issue. It's a long thread with many responses, but what was interesting was that opinion was also expressed regarding a certain supermarket that is connected to WalMart and the price of their food, the possible salary of a WalMart employee, and mickey-taking about the company's meet-and-greet policies for the under-95s. There was also commentary on a librarian's position regarding photocopying legislation and whether a WalMart employee would know about copyright legislation or even care about it. And that's a lot of information about how the public perceive Walmart, and the issues surrounding the services it provides. See Figures 3.18 and 3.19.

An article in the *Independent* newspaper describes how Goldman Sachs was accused of spreading rumours about rivals (Figure 3.20).[4]

Even the big players can be affected by rumours or be the perpetrators of them.

**Figure 3.18** The BoingBoing blog (1)

**Figure 3.19** The BoingBoing blog (2)

**Figure 3.20** Article by Stephen Foley on the Independent newspaper website

## Trade journals

Don't forget the trade journals. *Derivatives Week, Institutional Investor, Business Week, Private Eye, Business Times,* the *Financial News* and many more have gossip columns. I enjoy reading these, as some of the reports are hilarious. Awards dinners and other social events are reported here, along with the major names in business. Again, *Private Eye* will not mince its words when reporting on its investigations, which are global. The paper has ended up in court for libel on a number of occasions for hard-hitting reporting, but it doesn't deter staff from issuing their reportage of dodgy deals for its avid readers. *Private Eye* (*http://www.private-eye.co.uk*) is read by the general public, business population and governments alike.

### In the City

*With Slicker: "It is surprising to find Antigua is still home to a little known but fast-growing private wealth management and investment banking group which claims more than $50billion under management and more than $7billion in deposits. Little known, that is, until June when its sole owner, Texan-born banker Sir Allen Stanford, was beamed down onto the sacred green of Lord's, home of the MCC, with a Perspex container filled with $20m to announce his plans for '20/20' cricket."*

As we now know, Stanford was exposed as a fraudster, but *Private Eye* was already on his trail.[5]

## RSS feeds

Subscribe to industry RSS feeds and keep a check on what is being printed about the company. Vary your sources by pulling in data from various regions the company operates in, for example the Silk Road International Blog (*http://silkroadintl.net/blog/*) (Figure 3.21).

- Are they operating in any countries that are graded as low on the Transparency International Corruption Perceptions Index (see Chapter 4, 'Terrorism, surveillance and corruption')?

- Are there any broker reports for the company or the industry or industries in which they operate? Which analyst is writing the report? Are there any conflicting reports?

- What about their credit rating? Can you locate one? You may need to pay for this information, but the large business vendors can provide access to huge databases where this data is stored.

- Your sources of information must be reliable.

**Figure 3.21** The Silk Road International Blog

## Keep a record of the detail

It is important to retain an eye for the detail. Don't ignore anything, however insignificant it appears. Keep a record of it, as you may need to go back and check again. Your grid could end up looking something like the form shown in Figure 3.22.

This type of research can be as detailed as you need it to be. The end result is that you have done a thorough check on your potential customer and have complete insight into their operations, their business as a whole, their ethics and their people. You are now in a stronger position to make decisions.

**Figure 3.22** Sample form to keep track of the information you uncover

| XYZ Corporation – Initial Customer Identification |
|---|
| Date_____ Last updated_____ By_____ |
| Private and confidential |

| Description | Information | Identified | Information sources |
|---|---|---|---|
| Detailed analysis on how XYZ is perceived | Detailed breakdown | | |
| Summary | | | |
| HQ | 123 Corporation Building, | Y | Website – add hyperlink |
| Subsidiaries | 1a, 2a, 3a | Y | Website – add hyperlink |
| Business descriptions | Agriculture, GM foods, pesticides | Y | Website – add hyperlink |
| Mission statement | | Y | Website – add hyperlink |
| Public listed | LSE, NYSE, JSE, HKEx | Y | Website – add hyperlink |
| AR | Year ended 2008 | Y | Website – add hyperlink |
| Share price | Date | Y | Exchange websites – add hyperlinks |
| Broker reports | Analyst and company | N | Databases checked |
| Credit rating: S&Ps | Date | Y | Credit rating and forecast |
| **Leaders** | | | |
| CEO Directors Heads of finance, tax, legal, research | Names | Y | Sources |
| Litigation | Date | N | Cases and outcomes |
| Press and blogs, lists | Rumours | | List all with hyperlinks |
| Ongoing RSS feeds | comments | | List all |
| Notes | | | |

If you are checking individuals, the process is the same, but you would want to include information such as date of birth, residence and employment history to ensure you are researching the correct person. Use local press and social networking tools and look for them in places such as LinkedIn, Orkut, Plaxo, Namz and other professional networking sites. Don't forget that there are companies that specialise in employee background checks.

Some final words on this subject: Keep It Legal! Maintain your high ethical standards of professionalism. If you can't get to the information without breaking the law, don't do it. Put a question mark beside it. That's also your reputation on the line. If you are checking them, they are doing the same with you. What is your organisation's perceived reputation? Look it up. Find out what is being written and make it an ongoing routine to listen out for any rumours of your own.

# List of websites mentioned in this chapter

Awareness Watch™ Newsletter *http://www.awarenesswatch.com/*
BIS *http://www.bis.org/*
Blogspot *http://cybercases.blogspot.com/2008/01/how-to-avoid-10-worst-internet-scams-in.html*
BoingBoing *http://www.boingboing.net*
Corporate Investigations India *http://www.corporateinvestigationsindia.com/*
DMOZ *http://www.dmoz.org/Society/Issues/Fraud/Internet/*
FATF *http://www.fatf-gafi.org/*
FraudWatch International *http://www.fraudwatchinternational.com/*
Goldman Sachs *http://www2.goldmansachs.com/*
Independent newspaper *http://www.independent.co.uk*
Information Age *http://www.information-age.com/*
JPMorgan Chase *http://www.jpmorganchase.com/*
Kroll *http://www.kroll.com/services/screening/krs/*
National Consumers' League for Internet Fraud *http://www.fraud.org/internet/inttip/inttip.htm*
Nobody's Business *http://www.theglobeandmail.com/blogs/nobodysbusiness*
Private Eye *http://www.private-eye.co.uk/*
Silk Road International Blog *http://silkroadintl.net/blog/*
World News Network *http://www.wn.com/*
WorldLII *http://www.worldlii.org/*
World-newspapers.com *http://www.world-newspapers.com/world-news.html*

# Notes

1. India Cyber Law & Cases, 'How to avoid the 10 worst internet scams in 2008', at *http://cybercases.blogspot.com/2008/01/how-to-avoid-10-worst-internet-scams-in.html*.
2. JPMorgan Chase, 'Internet fraud and identity theft', at *http://www.jpmorganchase.com/cm/ContentServer?c=TS_Content&pagename=jpmorgan%2Fts%2FTS_Content%2FGeneral&cid=1123021915423*.
3. Pete Swabey, 'The inside job', *Information Age*, 13 August 2007, at *http://www.information-age.com/briefing-rooms/security-and-continuity/latest/273326/the-inside-job.thtml*.
4. Stephen Foley, 'Goldman accused of spreading rumours about rivals', *Independent*, 17 July 2008, at *http://www.independent.co.uk/news/business/news/goldman-accused-of-spreading-rumours-about-rivals-869809.html*.
5. *http://www.private-eye.co.uk*; see also Ian Rowley, 'Stanford fraud scandal: stumped by Sir Allen', *Business Week*, 18 February 2009, at *http://www.businessweek.com/globalbiz/blog/eyeonasia/archives/2009/02/sir_allen_and_m.html*.

# 4

# Terrorism, surveillance and corruption

## Monitoring terrorism

All around the world terrorism is an active, albeit destructive element of life. Terrorists do not discriminate by race, colour, gender, age, class, politics or religion. All are targets of the terrorist.

Much has been written on this subject by specialists in the field, and we are going to take a look at some of the information that is available to researchers on this topic. We are looking for information available to the public, not the intelligence community specialists.

Let's start by looking for quality information that is freely available. We won't be looking for specialist databases; those are the domain of the experts. However, there is a surprisingly large amount of excellent information in the public domain.

I was curious to see how many keywords I could locate on terrorism and related subjects. Here are just a few of them. Visualise making another mind map: terrorism: political, cyber/cyberwar/cyber warfare, operation, networks, cells, tracker/tracking, women in terrorism, intrusion, penetration, infiltration, international, defence, warfare, extremist/ extremism, domestic, electronic espionage (e-espionage), economic or industrial espionage, counter-surveillance, security, political freedom, risk assessment, terrornaut, dark web, atomic suicide bombing, sleeper cell, intelligence, civil disorder, radicalism, corruption, money laundering, know-your-customer, human trafficking.

### Anonymous searching

Sometimes you may want to use specific tools for this research in order to hide your Internet Protocol (IP) address from others. There are a number of tools that can assist with this function and many data security services are available that are free or pay for, offering anonymous searching.

### Anonymouse: *http://anonymouse.org/*

Anonymouse is a free web-based data security service enabling users to decide what information should be available to others about themselves, and in what circumstances. Anonymouse redirects your traffic via its own servers to obtain anonymity. On the downside, I found using Anonymouse made the browser slower to react. See Figure 4.1.

### About.com: *http://websearch.about.com/od/searchingtheweb/a/anonymous.htm*

About.com offers a comprehensive explanation in its Anonymous Surfing 101 series with product information about other services that are available. See Figure 4.2.

### Intute: *http://www.intute.ac.uk/*

We had another look at the databases of Intute to see what was on offer on this subject. One entry on its blog on terrorism (*http://www.intute .ac.uk/blog/2008/04/16/terrorism-in-the-limelight/*) states:

> Intute: Arts and Humanities looks at the background to these violent acts in the twentieth century in a new Limelight presentation

**Figure 4.1**  Anonymouse home page

## Figure 4.2    About.com web search page

## Figure 4.3    Article on terrorism on Intute

called History of Modern Terrorism in the West. As well as this historical and philosophical treatment of the subject Intute: Social Sciences has reviewed many hundreds of internet resources – you can browse thesauri for websites relating to terrorism and search for counter-terrorism, and browse for specific regional issues such as International Security, North America.

See Figure 4.3.

### Neil Doyle: *http://www.neildoyle.com/*

Neil Doyle, the ITV News terrorism specialist, is the author of a number of books on terrorism. See Figures 4.4 and 4.5.

The headlines on this site are free to access; however, to view an entire article is only possible if you pay for a subscription-based service. But if you drop a chosen headline into a search engine, the full article is accessible from the original publisher.

Looking further afield, I located a commentary from The Internet Patrol on hacking:

Hacking and politics have contrived to make strange bedfellows. According to a report by the British news organization, The Sun, hackers have come forward and started to take down websites which are fomenting terrorism, and inciting terrorist acts – something which the government cannot do with any sort of haste, if at all.

**Figure 4.4**  Information about the Neil Doyle Agency on the Neil Doyle website

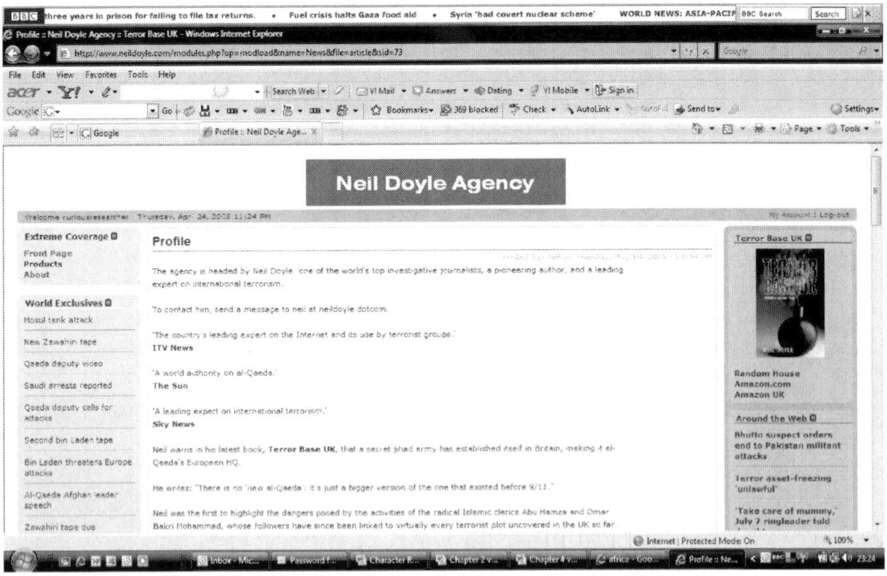

**Figure 4.5**   The home page of the Neil Doyle website

Neil Doyle, a British investigative journalist, and author of the book *Terror Tracker*, explained that 'The role of patriotic hackers in taking down extremists websites is clouded in deep secrecy, as it is illegal,' adding that 'The simple rule of thumb is that if a site has gone down quickly, maybe within minutes or hours after first being identified, it's likely to be hackers. Hosting companies and the authorities are usually slow to react and often nothing can be done, unless there's been a clear breach of the law.'

Many believe that al-Qaeda is using the Internet to communicate with cells, foment unrest and terrorist activities, and recruit new members – and quite successfully by all accounts.

Doyle said that it is also believed that al-Qaeda's master hacker has been operating out of London for some time. 'Britain is al-Qaeda's central communications hub and much of its online activities are co-ordinated from here,' he said.

There was a time when the UK was also considered prime real estate for hosting hate and terror websites, however as pressure has grown on the web hosting providers to take down such sites, many of the sites have moved to web hosting providers in the United States where, The Sun reports, 'the Federal Bureau of Investigation

(FBI) says that it would be "unconstitutional" and against the US constitution's First Amendment on freedom of speech if they were to pressure the hosting companies.'

Oh, the irony.[1]

## Government security agencies

It is also possible to subscribe to updates from government security agencies, such as MI5 (*https://www.mi5.gov.uk/output/Page16.html*) (Figure 4.6) and FBI (*http://www.fbi.gov/*) (Figure 4.7).

### Counterterrorism Blog: *http://counterterrorismblog.org/*

Further search brought me to Counterterrorism Blog, which is an amazing gateway to information aimed at policy makers and researchers. This blog is a goldmine of information, taking you off on tangents you hadn't necessarily expected to be following. There is a long list of terrorism experts who make contributions to the blog. There is a list of other related organisations, such as the Counterterrorism Foundation. The updated news articles take you on to coverage on many topics, including money laundering for funding terrorism. From there you can find your way to the Financial Action Task Force (FATF).

**Figure 4.6**  Information about threats on the MI5 website

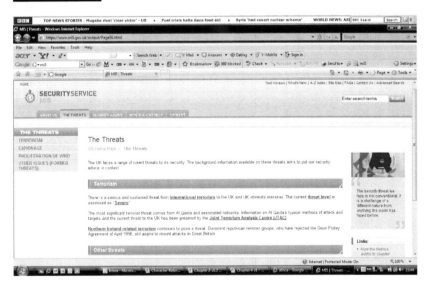

**Figure 4.7** Information about FBI 100 on the FBI website

Articles come from good sources, such as the *Washington Post*, Reuters, CBS and Jane's. There are expert reports created by the writers contributing to the blog, YouTube film from the National Archives, articles from Jane's, and many translations of terrorist messages from all over the globe. There is a huge list of websites and centres for researchers to explore for further information. Many hours can be spent just searching through this one absorbing resource. See Figure 4.8.

### The Information Warfare Site: *http://www.iwar.org.uk/index.htm*

There is also some very good information on the Information Warfare Site (IWS). This site aims to be an essential research centre for those interested in information security and operations. There is a section on psychological operations, with a definition of the term and many research papers and guidelines. See Figure 4.9.

### Association of Southeast Asian Nations: *http://www.aseansec.org/4964.htm*

Further afield, the Association of Southeast Asian Nations (ASEAN) has a section covering transnational crime and international terrorism. The website provides access to joint communiqués, press releases, declarations and other documents on combating terrorism in the region. See Figure 4.10.

**Figure 4.8**    A blog by Jeffrey Breinholt on the Counterterrorism Blog

**Figure 4.9**    The IWS home page

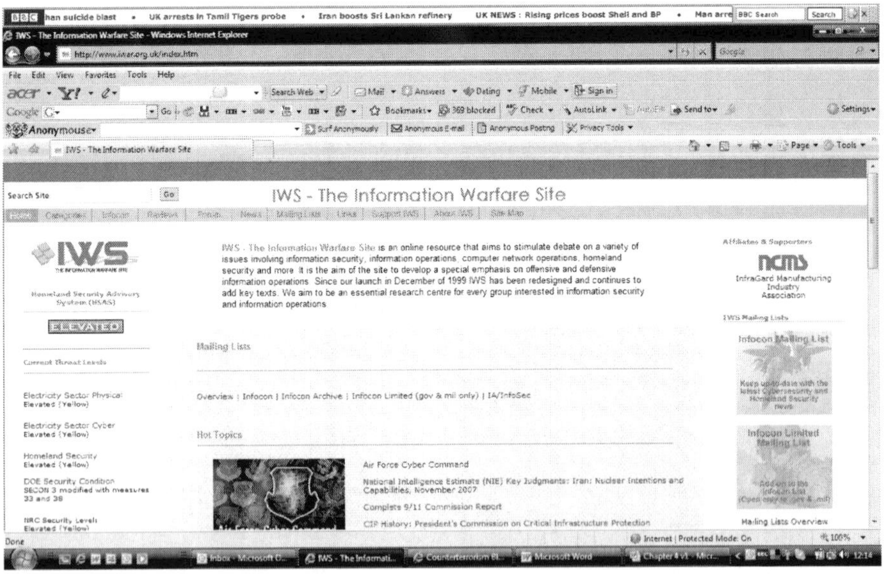

**Figure 4.10**  Information about transnational crime and international terrorism on the ASEAN website

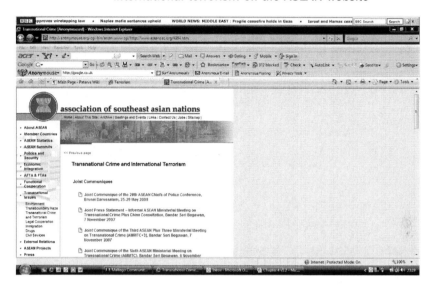

## Southeast Regional Centre for Counter-Terrorism: *http://www .searcct.gov.my/site1/*

The Malaysian Government set up the Southeast Regional Centre for Counter-Terrorism (SEARCCT) in 1992. The website concentrates on developing training courses in the Asian region, but also provides a list of other useful organisations. See Figure 4.11.

## Australian Transaction Reports and Analysis Centre: *http://www .austrac.gov.au/technical_assistance_and_training.html*

The Australian government provides information via the Australian Transaction Reports and Analysis Centre (AUSTRAC). The website includes information on the co-operative work undertaken in the region, including financing, databases and money laundering projects. There is information on research and business and regulatory issues. See Figure 4.12.

## Inter-American Committee Against Terrorism: *http://www.cicte .oas.org/Rev/en/*

South America is covered by the Inter-American Committee Against Terrorism (IACAT/CICTE). The website provides some good

**Figure 4.11** The home page of the SEARCCT website

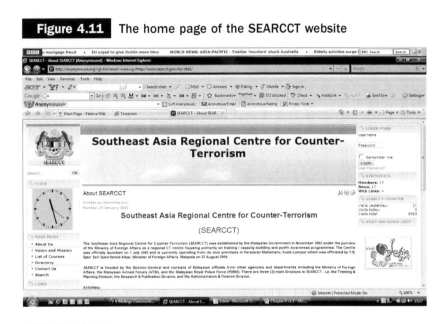

**Figure 4.12** Information about technical assistance and training on the AUSTRAC website

information for the region, such as documentation, news, policy, events and links to other organisations.

The 1947 Inter-American Treaty of Reciprocal Assistance, the 'Rio Treaty', was signed by 24 Latin American countries in Rio de Janeiro. Its purpose is to 'prevent and repel threats and acts of aggression against any countries of America'. See *http://www.oas.org/juridico/English/ treaties/b-29.html*.

The Trans-Sahara Counter Terrorism Initiative (TSCTI) is a US government inter-agency plan to address terrorist threats in Africa. There is no website for this US-funded initiative, but you can read more about TSCTI at About.com; see *http://terrorism.about.com/od/globalwaronterror/ p/TSCTI.htm*.

## EU Europa site on freedom, security and justice:
*http://ec.europa.eu/justice_home/fsj/terrorism/strategies/ fsj_terrorism_strategies_counter_en.htm*

The section on freedom, security and justice on the European Union's Europa website is detailed and available in different languages (Figures 4.13 and 4.14). The EU has created a counter-terrorism strategy which is available in pdf format.

The site covers many different aspects of counter-terrorism, for example the rights of children, asylum, immigration, police co-operation, customs, organised crime and more. It is a huge repository for researchers.

**Figure 4.13** Section on freedom, security and justice on the Europa website (1)

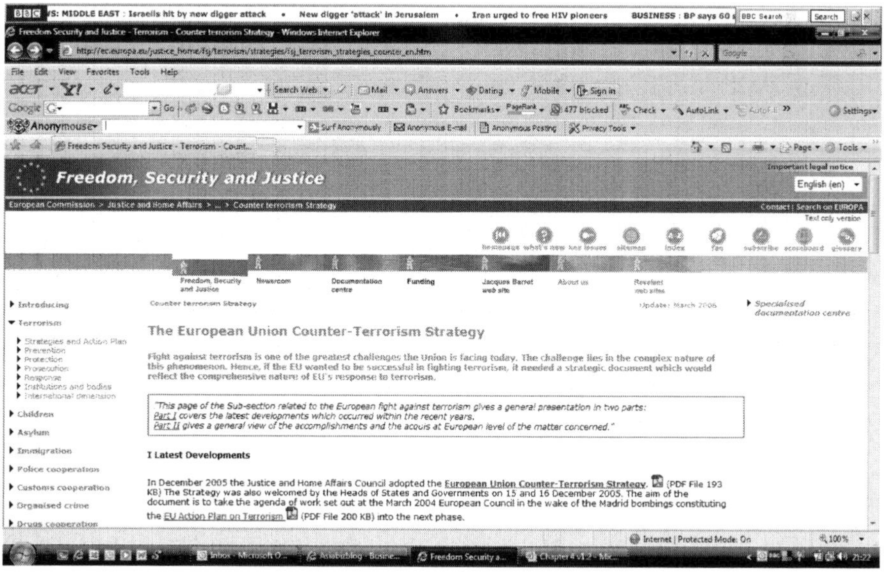

**Figure 4.14** Section on freedom, security and justice on the Europa website (2)

The Jamestown Foundation: *http://www.jamestown.org/terrorism/about.php*

The Jamestown Foundation, a Washington-based organisation, specifically addresses al-Qaeda and the war on terrorism on its website. It has global coverage and publishes timely updates by region. Jamestown claims to have a niche in this area by providing extensive translations and assessments of jihad on the web. See Figure 4.15.

## Censorship and propaganda

The global press is useful for gathering a balanced view on censorship and propaganda. Some countries may be very selective about what is published – or not published – or in other instances withdrawn by governments that do not like the content of a particular material and make it inaccessible.

The *Far Eastern Economic Review* (*FEER*) was banned from sale in China in June 2008 (Figure 4.16). This demonstrates the importance of gathering a mixed bag of information from global sources. In July 2008

**Figure 4.15** Information about Jamestown's terrorism program on the Jamestown Foundation website

**Figure 4.16** The home page of the FEER website

*FEER* published a fabulous article called 'China's guerrilla war for the web'.[2]

The Chinese Communist Party views the power of the internet as a medium to be exploited for propaganda. The Party employs students to monitor blogs and make entries that are pro-Party policy, thereby silencing any anti-communist dissenters – according to FEER, what President Hu Jintao called 'a new pattern of public opinion guidance'. He also said the Party 'needed to use the internet as well as control it'.

### Reporters Without Borders: *http://www.rsf.org*

Reporters Without Borders is an agency that champions freedom of speech and challenges censorship in the press. The website has global coverage and includes internet freedom. See Figure 4.17.

## Cyber terrorism

I came across a very detailed article published in April 2007 in *Information Age* by Pete Swabey called 'Cyber assault'.[3] It highlights the growing worries that the corporate and business community face from attack by hackers. The article demonstrates the growing vulnerability of the utilities, oil and gas companies, airlines and other industries as they merge with each other, and in the process weaken their IT platforms, opening them up to potential external abuse. The technical capabilities of the hackers have grown in strength with no shortage of those willing

**Figure 4.17** The home page of the Reporters Without Borders website

to exploit companies' data for a multitude of reasons, including industrial espionage. The author then provides examples of how an organisation can repulse external attacks, and protect its internal data assets. Although pointed at UK industries, the issues this article addresses affect companies globally. There are other equally good articles on this subject provided by *Information Age*.

PriceWaterhouseCoopers (PwC; *http://www.pwc.com/*) produces a regular Economic Crime Survey at *http://www.pwc.com/extweb/home .nsf/docid/29CAE5B1F1D40EE38525736A007123FD* and other reports relating to global espionage, counterfeiting, pirating and the theft of intellectual property, trade secrets and other assets. There are supplemental videos and reports based on regions and industries such as the chemical industry, engineering and construction, industrial manufacturing, retail and consumer, transport and logistics.

I located a short film where Chinese hackers claim to have been paid by the Chinese government to hack into high-level private and government websites, including the Pentagon (*http://www.skipease.com/ blog/hacker/chinese-hackers-claim-breaking-into-pentagon-website/*) (Figure 4.18).

**Figure 4.18**   Information about Chinese hackers breaking into the Pentagon website on Skipease

# Defence research

## *Surveillance: defence research*

There are many areas of defence research that the average person would not be able to access unless they worked for the military, armed forces, aerospace or security agencies. There is a massive hive of hidden activity that the public can only guess at. There are organisations which cater for specialist interest groups for information professionals. As an example, the Chartered Institute of Library and Information Professionals (CILIP) has a Defence and Surveillance Group and the Special Libraries Association (SLA) has a Defence and Military Librarians Group. Access to these specialist areas is only allowed to members, who can participate in the discussion groups and blogs. Social networking is heavily used as a vital tool for investigating all forms of potential criminal and terrorist activity.

### The Dark Web Terrorism Research Project:
*http://ai.arizona.edu/research/terror/index.htm*

Surveillance comes in many guises. The University of Arizona Artificial Intelligence Lab has launched the Dark Web Terrorism Research Project to use computers to combat terrorism:

> The AI Lab Dark Web project is a long-term scientific research program that aims to study and understand the international terrorism (Jihadist) phenomena via a computational, data-centric approach. We aim to collect 'ALL' web content generated by international terrorist groups, including websites, forums, chat rooms, blogs, social networking sites, videos, virtual world, etc.

See Figure 4.19.

The project also provides access to a number of scholarly research publications, which include references to other sources of information where you can deviate from your trail. Figure 4.20 shows an example.

I have also found it useful to contact the authors directly with questions.

## Who is watching whom?

While on the subject of surveillance, who is watching whom?

The BBC reported that Facebook and Google Earth were being used to track the location of war criminals and that the War Crimes Watch

**Figure 4.19** Information about the AI Lab Dark Web project on the University of Arizona website

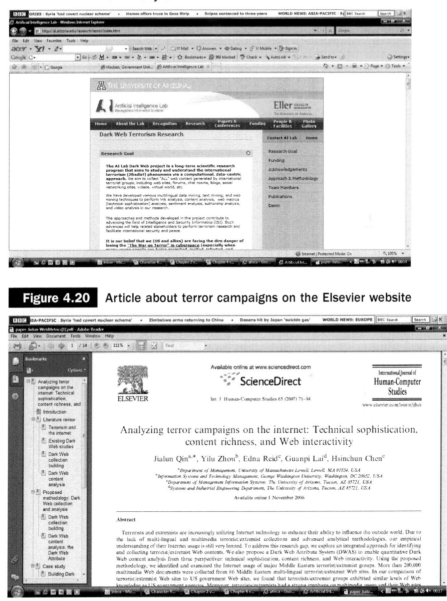

**Figure 4.20** Article about terror campaigns on the Elsevier website

List was asking people on Facebook to report sightings of certain people who were wanted on the list.[4]

Web 2.0 technologies, including social networking tools, play an important part in tracking information in many languages. Accurate translation of that information is vital to the intelligence retrieved by researchers.

## Intelligence retrieved by researchers

As part of their work, researchers gather large amounts of information about other people and make many contacts. Personal professional relationships are forged, but who owns this information and in what context has it been gathered? What about the person ordered by a UK court to divulge his contact list on FaceBook to his employers?

It is very important to make a distinction between those relationships and ensure they are strictly separated out. In the case Pennwell Publishing Ltd v Ornstein and others (*http://www.bailii.org/ew/cases/EWHC/QB/2007/1570.html*) there was a complicated argument regarding contractual terms and conditions, and a lack of restrictions involving moving data from one employer to another and adding in private contacts. The judge found for the claimant (Penwell) and their right to retain the data. Figure 4.21 shows the case on the website of the British and Irish Legal Information Institute (BAILII).

This case was reported in *The Register* in July 2007.[5] It was discussed on the companylawforum.co.uk. The Greater Manchester Police have launched an application on Facebook to gather public information on

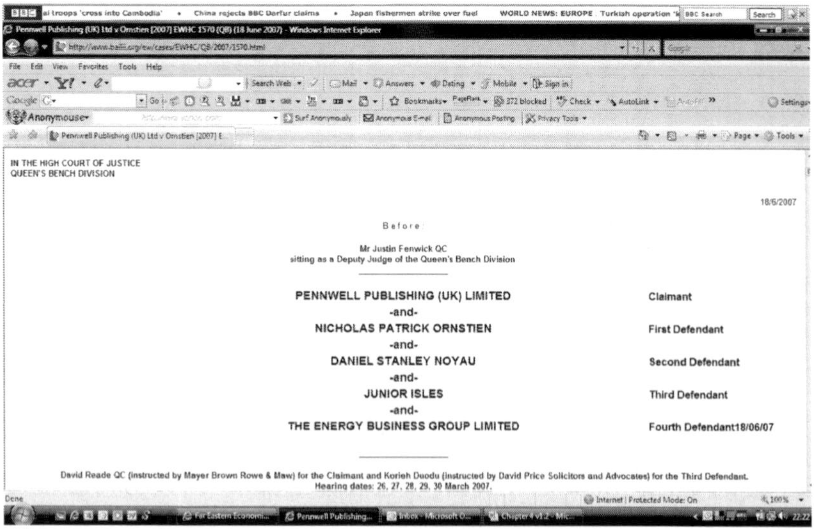

**Figure 4.21** Pennwell Publishing Ltd v Ornstein and others on the BAILII website

criminal activity.[6] They can also access the profiles of Facebook members.

## The role of librarians

What is the librarian's role in this area? According to an article in the *Bookseller*, police are now accessing the library borrowing records and internet search records of people they have under surveillance (Figure 4.22). The article says that this came to public attention in the US after the introduction of the US Patriot Act 2001, which caused controversy. It highlights points of concern for librarians in deciding what to stock and ensuring that literature that may be of interest to the terrorist population was not readily available. It also covers the stocking of religious materials.[7]

**Figure 4.22**  Article about the anti-terror threat on the Bookseller website

## Search engine companies

Search engine companies are also watching you. A record of every word typed into a search engine, every page browsed and every film clip uploaded is captured and stored for analysis.

This practice was challenged in 2008. A US court has ordered Google to hand over record logs to Viacom of data relating to YouTube films. It was finally agreed that Google would supply the data to Viacom with user ID data stripped out to protect user privacy (Figure 4.23).[8] The ramifications for user privacy breaches and IP address identification raised by this case are huge.

**Figure 4.23** Article about networking on the Guardian newspaper website

# Corruption

Corruption occurs when powerful persons in business lack integrity in their economic or political dealings, for example by obtaining or offering funding for dubious or illegal activities, either by bribery or backhanders. Governments, industries and those in powerful positions are all open to bribery, which is not in the best interests of those they represent.

## Measuring corruption

Corruption can and is being measured. No organisation or body with a reputation they value would enter into any business dealings with a country, organisation or company without checking who they are dealing with. The ability of a country, organisation or company to demonstrate transparency and due diligence in their dealings is very important. See also Chapter 3, 'Do you know your customer?'

- The original intention of the United Nations Oil-for-Food Programme in Iraq was to provide food and medicine for the Iraqi people in exchange for their oil. The programme was exposed by Paul Volker and his team to show a huge network of illicit deals, where some of the oil money ended up in the pockets of Iraqi government ministers and UN officials. The programme was shut down in 2003.

- Bradford & Bingley lost Resolution as an investor after it refused them access to its books as part of Resolution's due diligence exercise. Bradford & Bingley was over-exposed to the sub-prime loans market via GMAC in its effort to expand its business. Bradford & Bingley still has obligations to buy more loans from GMAC.

- BAE Systems was involved in Serious Fraud Office investigations over bribery claims with its supply of arms to Saudi Arabia's Al Yammamah. It was also accused of bribery, corruption and fraud in six other countries.

## Corruption statistics

There are corruption indices where researchers can check the corruption perception by country.

### Transparency International: *http://www.transparency.org/*

Transparency International (TI) has published an annual Corruption Perception Index since 1994 (*http://www.transparency.org/policy_research/surveys_indices/cpi/2007*) (Figure 4.24). Part of its methodology for gathering data is to use experts from risk analysis agencies, country risk analysts, residents, non-residents, business leaders, a confidence range and data from many organisations such as the Asian Development Bank. TI's report is the highest respected measurement of perceived corruption.

In 2007 Denmark ranked highest, with a clean score of 9.4; bottom of the list was Somalia, with a score of 1.4.

TI also provides access to corruption reports by industry and a bribe payers' index. There's much more information available from its home page, and TI's statistics are quoted on the World Bank and IMF websites and many others.

**Figure 4.24** The Corruption Perception Index on the Transparency International website

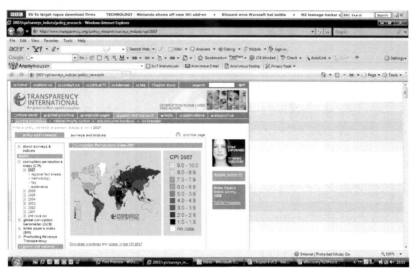

TI has alliances with other corruption organisations such as the Internet Center for Corruption Research (ICCR) at the University of Passau (*http://www.icgg.org/corruption.index.html*). The ICCR organises an annual programme called 'The Economics of Corruption: Studying Anticorruption at the University Level'.

The Bulgarian AntiCorruption Portal (*http://www.anticorruption.bg/index_eng.php*) provides corruption statistics, with the latest data being from 2005.

## Corruption blogs

Don't forget to check out some of the many corruption blogs that are available. Topics vary enormously. These are just a few of them:

- *http://blogs.america.gov/democracy/2008/06/13/the-toxic-triangle-of-drugs-corruption-and-violence/*

- *http://blogs.reuters.com/africa/tag/corruption/*

- *http://blogs.reuters.com/africa/tag/corruption/SitePK:1740530,00.html*

- *http://web.worldbank.org/WBSITE/EXTERNAL/WBI/EXTWBIGOVANTCOR/0,,contentMDK:21685370~menuPK:1740542~pagePK:64168445~piPK:64168309~th*

- *http://www.chinalawblog.com/2008/06/the_upside_of_china_corruption
  .html*
- *http://www.taxresearch.org.uk/Blog/2007/09/18/world-bank-targets-
  corruption-in-havens/*
- *http://www.thenation.com/blogs/capitalgames?bid=3&pid=228339*

## Money laundering

### The Financial Action Task Force: *http://www.fatf-gafi.org/pages/ 0,3417,en_32250379_32235720_1_1_1_1_1,00.html*

The Financial Action Task Force on Money Laundering (FATF) was created in 1989 to combat money laundering and the financing of terrorist activities. It has published 40 + 9 separate recommendations to achieve its objectives. FATF currently has 34 member countries and two observer countries, and works regionally with other associated members. Its work includes collaborating with other FATF-style regional bodies and a long list of organisations from areas specialising in banking, securities, drugs, money laundering and Interpol. See Figure 4.25.

There are many working papers, theses and articles covering corruption research available from organisations and academic institutions. Add 'poverty' as a related search term to enhance the results.

**Figure 4.25** The home page of the FATF website

The websites covered in this chapter will keep the interested reader browsing hundreds of related topics for many hours.

# List of websites mentioned in this chapter

Anonymous Surfing 101 *http://websearch.about.com/od/searchingtheweb/ a/anonymous.htm*

Anonymouse *http://anonymouse.org/*

Association of Southeast Asian Nations (ASEAN) *http://www.aseansec .org/4964.htm*

Australian Transaction Reports and Analysis Centre (AUSTRAC) *http://www.austrac.gov.au/technical_assistance_and_training.html*

BAILII *http://www.bailii.org*

BBC *http://news.bbc.co.uk*

The Bookseller magazine *http://www.thebookseller.com/*

Bulgarian AntiCorruption Portal *http://www.anticorruption.bg/index_eng .php*

Counterterrorism Blog *http://counterterrorismblog.org/*

Dark Web Terrorism Research *http://ai.arizona.edu/research/terror/ index.htm*

Europa site on freedom, security and justice *http://ec.europa.eu/justice_home/ fsj/terrorism/strategies/fsj_terrorism_ strategies_counter_en.htm*

Far East Economic Review *http://www.feer.com/*

FBI *http://www.fbi.gov/*

Financial Action Task Force on Money Laundering *http://www.fatf-gafi .org/*

Google Earth *http://earth.google.com/*

Guardian newspaper *http://www.guardian.co.uk*

Information Age *http://www.information-age.com/*

Information Warfare Site *http://www.iwar.org.uk/index.htm*

Inter-American Committee Against Terrorism (IACAT/CICTE) *http:// www.cicte.oas.org/Rev/en/*

Internet Center for Corruption Research *http://www.icgg.org/corruption .index.html*

Internet Patrol *http://www.theinternetpatrol.com/*

Intute blog on terrorism *http://www.intute.ac.uk/blog/2008/04/16/terrorism-in-the-limelight/*

Jamestown Foundation *http://www.jamestown.org/terrorism/about .php*

MI5 *https://www.mi5.gov.uk/output/Page16.html*
Neil Doyle Agency *http://www.neildoyle.com/*
PricewaterhouseCoopers *http://www.pwc.com/*
The Register *http://www.the register.co.uk/*
Reporters Without Borders *http://www.rsf.org/*
Rio Treaty *http://www.oas.org/juridico/English/treaties/b-29.html*
Skipease *http://www.skipease.com*
Southeast Regional Centre for Counter-Terrorism (SEARCCT) *http://www.searcct.gov.my/site1/*
Transparency International *http://www.transparency.org/*
Trans-Sahara Counterterrorism Initiative via About *http://terrorism.about.com/od/globalwaronterror/p/TSCTI.htm*

## Blogs

China Law Blog *http://www.chinalawblog.com/*
Facebook *http://www.facebook.com/login.php*
The Nation Blog *http://www.thenation.com/blogs*
Reuters *http://blogs.reuters.com/*
Social Networking Tax Research *http://www.taxresearch.org.uk/Blog*
US Government *http://blogs.america.gov/democracy/*

## Notes

1. The Internet Patrol, 'Hackers, government unite to take down terrorist websites', 27 July 2005, at *http://www.theinternetpatrol.com/hackers-government-unite-to-take-down-terrorist-websites*.
2. David Bandurski, 'China's guerrilla war for the web', *Far Eastern Economic Review*, July 2008, at *http://www.feer.com/essays/2008/august/chinas-guerrilla-war-for-the-web*.
3. Pete Swabey, 'Cyber assault', *Information Age*, 21 April, 2007, at *http://www.information-age.com/briefing-rooms/security-and-continuity/latest/273361/cyber-assault.thtml*.
4. BBC News, 'Facebook to track Darfur suspects', 25 April 2008, at *http://news.bbc.co.uk/2/hi/africa/7367634.stm*.
5. See *http://www.theregister.co.uk/2007/07/16/social_networking_profiles_company_property*.
6. Greater Manchester Police, 'Greater Manchester Police uses Facebook to crack crime', at *http://www.gmp.police.uk/mainsite/pages/1591DCCE9694D4B48025742D004CDE8D.htm*.

7. Benedicte Page, 'Anti-terror threat to librarian role', *Bookseller*, 2 May 2008, at *http://www.thebookseller.com/news/57851-anti-terror-threat-to-librarian-role.html*.

8. John Naughton, 'Who might be keeping watch on what you are watching?', *Guardian*, 13 July 2008, at *http://www.guardian.co.uk/media/2008/jul/13/googlethemedia.virginmedia*.

# 5

# Where next? What's new? Next generation social networking tools to enhance research outcomes

As our online interaction grows, so does the opportunity to exploit the information trail we leave behind us. It is like leaving footprints in the sand for others to follow. We are networking and conducting transactions with other people across the globe. Time zones have now become less of a barrier, as has the need to travel in order to interact in the business environment.

## Internet World Stats: *http://www.internetworldstats.com/*

Internet World Stats is an internet usage and population site providing data by region. See Figure 5.1.

Figure 5.2 shows how one can view and interpret internet usage statistics in Oceania by country and population.

We can select other regions and see the growth of country-by-country usage. Internet World Stats provides a blog, a glossary of technical terminology, an explanation of how staff compile the data and many other resources for tracking this information. See Figure 5.3.

## Privacy International: *http://www.privacyinternational.org/*

Privacy International (PI) takes a different stance: it monitors how search engines use the data they collect from searchers. See Figure 5.4.

It is concerned with many aspects of privacy, from fingerprinting, ID cards, terrorism and surveillance, and Big Brother Awards to the privacy practices of internet and Web 2.0 technologies and services. It has led campaigns against the practices of internet companies such as Amazon.

In 2007 it produced a report after a six-month investigation into the privacy practices of key internet-based companies and 'lists the ranking

**Figure 5.1** Internet usage statistics on Internet World Stats

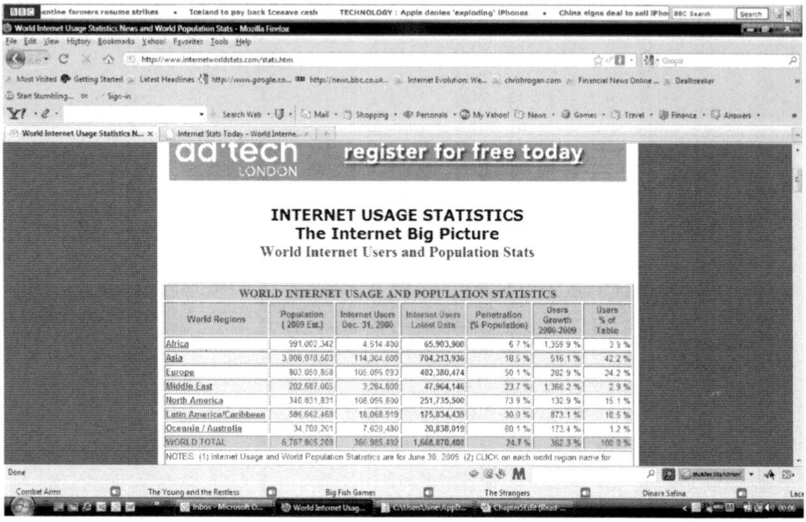

**Figure 5.2** Internet usage and population statistics for Oceania on Internet World Stats

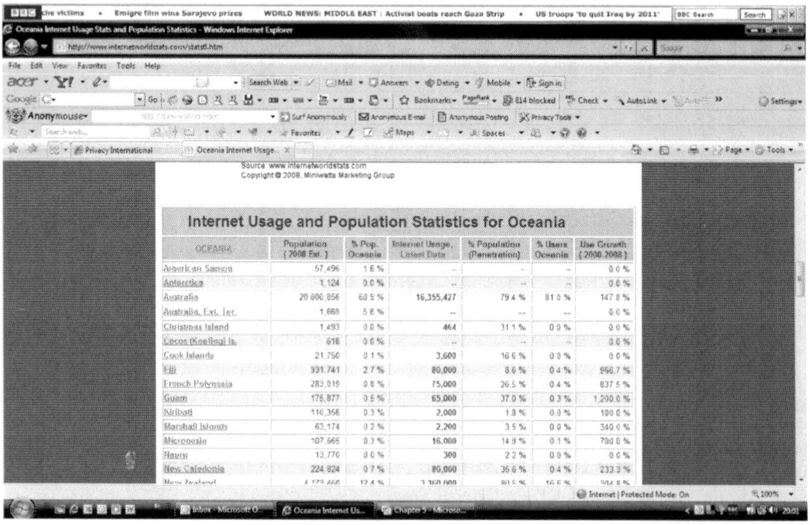

of the best and the worst performers both in Web 1.0 and Web 2.0 across the full spectrum of search, email, e-commerce and social networking sites'.[1] The report was conducted as concerns had been raised about the way internet companies handled personal information; it highlighted the

**Figure 5.3**    Other options on Internet World Stats

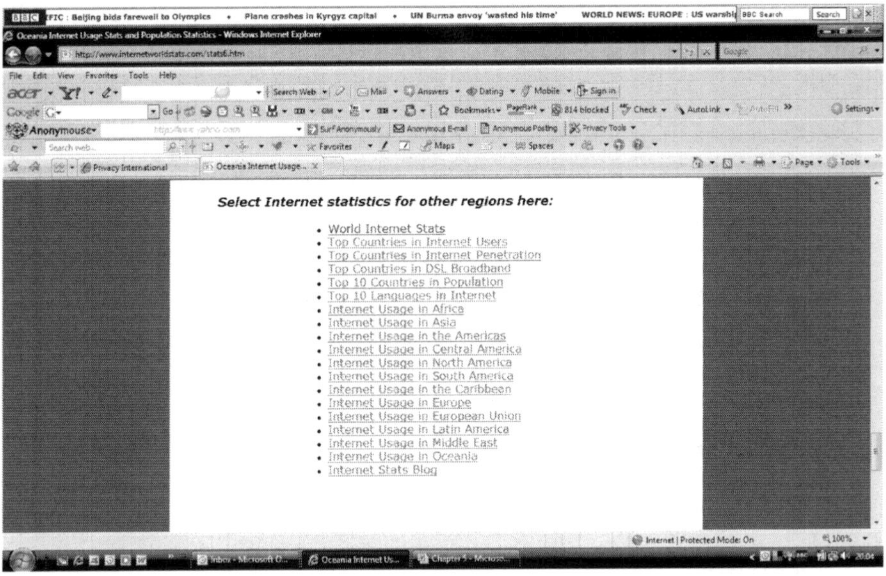

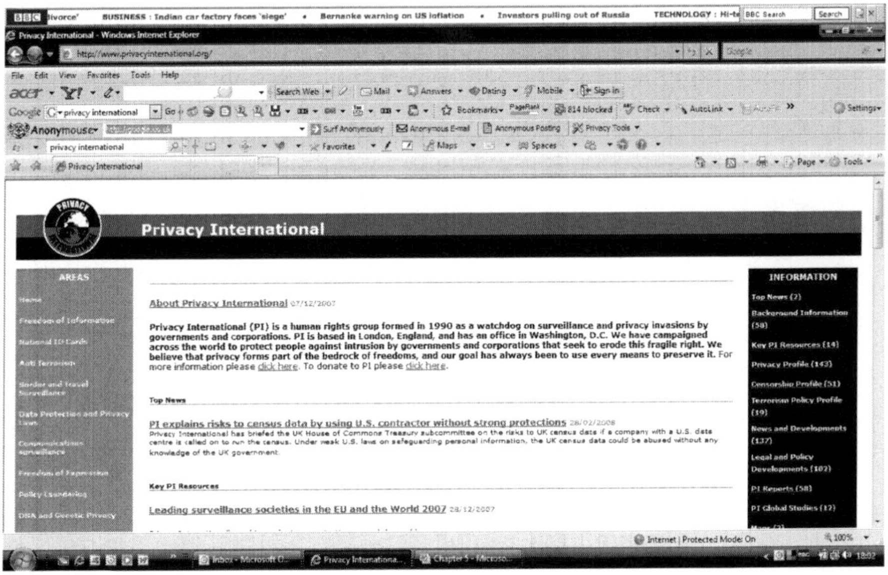

**Figure 5.4**    The home page of the Privacy International website

need to raise consumers' awareness about the way in which their data is used, to allow them to make a more informed decision before putting their information into the public domain.

These are some of the companies investigated in the consultation document:

- Amazon
- AOL
- Apple
- BBC
- Bebo
- eBay
- Facebook
- Friendster
- Google
- Hi5
- Last.fm
- LinkedIn
- LiveJournal
- Microsoft
- MySpace
- Orkut
- Reunion.com
- Skype™
- Wikipedia
- Windows Live Space
- Xanga
- Yahoo!
- YouTube

Google was placed at the bottom of the ranking because, in the words of PI, 'we have found numerous deficiencies and hostilities in Google's approach to privacy that go well beyond those of other organizations', and the report lists some of Google's privacy failures. PI ranked Microsoft higher on the list, but the report states that their practices, although not as contentious as those of Google, also have some black marks against them.

PI comes to the overall conclusion that the internet companies' privacy standards are appalling. At the end of the consultation document there are hyperlinks to some of PI's campaigns for more internet privacy and data use by the internet companies. This report is well worth reading before you put any more of your personal information out on the net.

# VoIP – Voice over Internet Protocol

VoIP is an internet protocol telephony service, offering a number of ways to communicate through a fast internet broadband connection. When one uses VoIP, if feels as if it is possible to hop from country to country, ignoring time zones, as long as your contacts are awake to interact with you.

There are many VoIP providers in the market, the best known one being Skype™ (*http://www.skype.com/intl/en-gb/*). I have been a big user of Skype™ for making contact for business purposes across the world at no cost, for making local calls when my phone line went down and for instant messaging (IM) to friends. I added a web cam and it was great to be able to talk to and see colleagues as far away as Australia. The quality of the communication has generally been very high, although I have experienced some disparity in the voice/image connectivity. VoIP offers the user the opportunity to upload contacts lists and videos to MySpace and other social networks. There is a lot of equipment available in the shops specifically for Skype™ and other VoIP users.

Some companies have brought this technology in-house as a much cheaper option to a main land line telephone network. However, others have reservations as to whether VoIP compromises corporate firewall defences. They err on the side of caution, watching their competitors, waiting for the possibility of a crack to emerge causing a possible loss of corporate data, mass spamming (SPIT – SPamming over Internet Telephony) or another invasion of their internal systems.

Another large VoIP provider, Vonage, was the target of phishing activity recently,[2] as reported by FraudWatch International (*http://www .fraudwatchinternational.com*), so these threats are very real (Figure 5.5).

Until recently, I hadn't given a huge amount of thought about the 'dark side' of this technology. When I received the communication

**Figure 5.5** A fake website shown on FraudWatch International

You are subscribed to FraudWatch International.
To discontinue your subscription use the link at the bottom of this message.

*FraudWatch International*   **FRAUD ALERT**

www.fraudwatchinternational.com

| Phishing Alerts | | | | | | |
|---|---|---|---|---|---|---|

***Phishing Site Statistics***

Current Active 4,831
Total Detected 469,154

***Report Email Fraud***

Nigerian 419 Scam Letters, Lottery emails, Phishing emails and other fraudulent emails should be forwarded to our Investigations Team at:
scams
@fraudwatchinternational.com

## Vonage – 'Customer Notice – ref-id#8987233'

| Date Issued: | Wednesday 27th August 2008 |
|---|---|
| Fraud Alert # | 225374 |
| Target Company: | Vonage |
| From Address: | auto-db@vonage.com |
| Subject Line: | Customer Notice – ref-id#8987233 |

Protect Your Online Identity

## Free FWI Membership for Law
**Enforcement and Financial Institutions.**
**Please Click here to Contact us to Apply**

## Phishing Methods Used:

| Email: | Deceptive Subject Line |
|---|---|
| | Forged Senders Address |
| | Genuine Looking Content |
| | Disguised Hyperlinks |

| Web Site: | Genuine Looking Content |
|---|---|
| | Form – Collection of Information |
| | Incorrect URL, not disguised |

A copy of the email is displayed below.

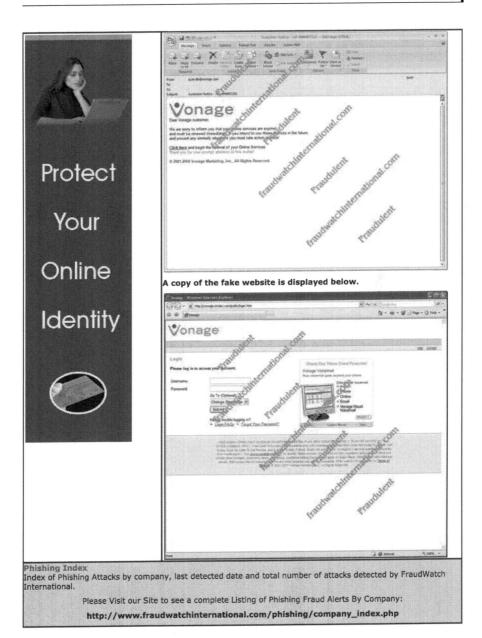

A copy of the fake website is displayed below.

**Phishing Index**
Index of Phishing Attacks by company, last detected date and total number of attacks detected by FraudWatch International.

Please Visit our Site to see a complete Listing of Phishing Fraud Alerts By Company:

**http://www.fraudwatchinternational.com/phishing/company_index.php**

**Figure 5.6**    Example of unscrupulous behaviour via Skype™ Chat

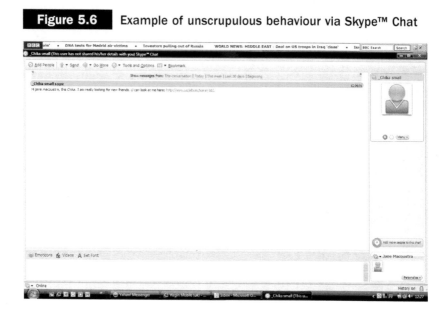

illustrated in Figure 5.6 I was disappointed and then irritated to see Skype™ being put to use in this unscrupulous manner.

Whoever had made this initial contact had shown the sleazy side of VoIP, clearly demonstrating that it is open to abuse just as much as any other internet Web 2.0 offering. I did not reply to 'xsexy18', nor to other similar communications, and you can block their advances.

One use for VoIP telephony that occurred to me a long time ago was that it could be used in schools or higher education to interact with other classrooms and share views and meet overseas students online to compare learning practices and cultural differences. Or how about the kid who is off school for the longer term; with a laptop and a web cam, they could still continue their studies remotely and interact with their teacher and classmates.

This community has not yet emerged in the education system in the UK, probably because the education system retains very strict firewalls about what can be accessed via the internet. How many of you have ever tried to do research from a public library computer? Forget it, and stick with the books. Distance learners in the higher education community are a big community who maintain contact with tutors and other students via e-mail and telephone, but as far as I am aware have not yet taken advantage of the benefits of using VoIP technology for classroom activities. It could be hugely beneficial.

# Protecting internal IT systems

Thousands of companies offer defence services to businesses for their internal IT systems to help them protect themselves from viruses, spyware and malware and other undesirables. One company, Sophos (*http://www.sophos.com*), produced the *Security Threat Report 2008*, which explains some of the ways that people can be targeted:

> Spear-phishers can easily generate the victims' addresses by using spammers' software that, for example, combines given names and family names. They might also have exploited a list of employees by finding a directory on a network such as Facebook or LinkedIn. And because the phishing emails are sent only to a single domain, it is less likely that they will appear on a security vendor's radar.[3]

See Figure 5.7.

Sophos also published a list called the Dirty Dozen (Figure 5.8):

> Brazil sees biggest increase, taking second place in the 'Dirty Dozen' of spam relaying countries
>
> IT security and control firm Sophos has published its latest report into the top twelve spam relaying countries, covering the first

**Figure 5.7**   The home page of the Sophos website

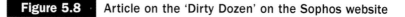

**Figure 5.8** Article on the 'Dirty Dozen' on the Sophos website

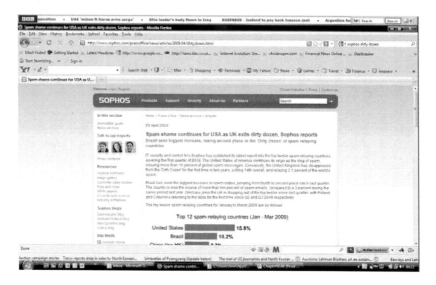

quarter of 2009. The United States of America continues its reign as the king of spam, relaying more than 15 percent of global spam messages. Conversely, the United Kingdom has disappeared from the 'Dirty Dozen' for the first time in two years, polling 14th overall, and relaying 2.1 percent of the world's spam.

Brazil has seen the biggest increase in spam output, jumping from fourth to second place since last quarter. The country is now the source of more than ten percent of spam emails, compared to 4.3 percent during the same period last year. Germany joins the UK in dropping out of the top twelve since last quarter, with Poland and Columbia returning to the table for the first time since Q2 and Q3 2008 respectively.[4]

# Social networking sites

Private profiles are public profiles – you use social networking to put information out in the public domain about yourself. That's fine. So do I and millions of others. However, I have started to join business networks where I can hide my profile from non-members and have worded my profile in such a way that when spidered, it won't easily be found by a search engine for this particular piece of information about me.

The search engine spiders (indexers) the first line only of my profile, so in one particular instance, I deliberately made it bland enough in the search keywords not to bring up my profile for the perusal of all, leaving the rest of my personal data sitting behind a login and password barrier. If you put your personal data out there, it can be located with enough patience and tenacity.

Actually, even if you don't put it out there, someone else does it for you. Imagine you're a 90 year old, who has trouble starting the video, let alone taking any notice of this new-fangled computer and internet stuff. Are your details going to be hidden from the world? No. Your name, address, telephone number, council tax, land registry data if you're a home owner and other data has been loaded into a database where someone can find you in one capacity or another. The government agencies know you exist, so it doesn't matter where your physical location is. Once you are in the system, you can be located. A researcher might need to pay for the information, but it's already out there for the taking.

Let me suggest to you that you had a wild night out with friends. You or your friends post some photos and all your names, maybe the name of your home town and the venue on YouTube, MySpace, Friendster, Hi5, Flickr, Badoo or any other similar social networking group. One of you is job hunting and attending interviews. The HR department of the company you really want to work for can locate your name and see photos of you out with your mates having a great time. How would you feel about that? What were you doing in the pictures? What comments were posted? Let's go back to ethics again. Is this ethical behaviour by the HR department? If not, why not? You or your friends put the photos and information out there to be looked at by others – by anybody. It is your right to have freedom of speech and freedom of expression; but it is the right of others to find that expression, with not much in place by way of barriers to how they use it, unless it is used for vindictive or spiteful purposes. You will be 'seen' as you have portrayed yourself, and so will your friends. People will draw their own opinions from the image you create for yourself. That's not necessarily a bad thing, as the work hard, play hard ethos could also probably be a hiring consideration in some organisations where their staff interact with each other out of the office as well as in it. The headhunter out hunting for potential stars of the future (in a business context) will also use social networks to gather information about people and build a profile.

Do you think that those listed on Fortune's 'Bosses behaving badly' list wanted to be on there? They didn't write this stuff about themselves, but the information was available for someone else to write it instead.

The portrayed image is important. Look at groups like the Women's Institute (*http://www.thewi.org.uk/*), as an example, who no longer want to be portrayed as the jam-making, knitting, sewing, gardening, do-gooder population of middle-class suburbia in the UK who stay at home instead of going to work. Do they look like that type of organisation now? They have changed direction by expanding their horizons with projects in other parts of the world. This work demonstrates their flexibility, which includes the projects that take them overseas. See Figure 5.9.

**Figure 5.9** The home page of the Women's Institute website

### YouTube: *http://www.youtube.com*

YouTube has dedicated country sites, so that people can post videos and images of themselves via their country site. Figure 5.10 shows the one for Japan – *http://jp.youtube.com/* – and the website can be translated into English. For quicker results use the 'inurl:' command in Google and the country suffix with the website name to locate YouTube in a specific country; it will save you time trawling through lists of results for the right hit.

There are some differences between the Japanese version and the English language translation (Figure 5.11).

I generally use YouTube for a bit of fun, and others have sent me some really good, very funny stuff. But YouTube has a more serious side and

**Figure 5.10** The Japanese country site of YouTube

**Figure 5.11** The English language translation of the Japanese country site of YouTube

is used for political exposure, training purposes and business and marketing. Google has used YouTube to load up demonstrations of its latest web browser, 'Chrome', which enables potential new users to view its specifications before they download the software (Figure 5.12). See

**Figure 5.12** YouTube loaded into the Google Chrome browser

*http://www.google.com/support/chrome/bin/answer.py?answer=95451&hl=en_GB.*

YouTube runs commercial advertisements from its site. The press release has morphed into a life form that spans the globe in nanoseconds as a video, web cam, SMS message, IM, RSS feed, rumour, blog, wiki or other type of electronic medium.

## Social networking tools aimed at the unwary innocent

The social networking technologies are, on one hand, a great way to find new people in business and for social networking purposes, and on the other, a honey pot for predators against the unwary innocent. A good example of the latter are the social networking tools aimed at children. There's a site that uses animals with names instead of people. My kids enjoyed using it to interact with their school mates online, participating in strategy games and sending each other messages. One day, they told me one of their animals had been banned for life from use. I contacted the proprietors and asked why this had happened. The response was that they had sent 'inappropriate content', which had been intercepted. They sent me a copy of the communication, which was a bit of an eyebrow-raiser seeing the worst expletives imaginable set out in a very inarticulate e-mail. It was apparent that someone in another continent and time zone had obtained access and used the account and the animals to send messages. I compared the message with that of another parent who found her son's animal had been exploited for the same purpose. The two animals had been interacting online via these children and many other school friends' animals. It appeared that an infiltration network had or was being built via a children's game. It should be the responsibility of these companies to ensure they create robust systems that cannot be so easily infiltrated by others.

As previously discussed, people download and are actively encouraged to download their entire social and/or business contact lists to these sites. Along with other personal information, it is made available to others, which compromises data integrity and ownership. If you consider how the police and other surveillance organisations use social networks for their research, it is understandable why these networks are such valuable tools when placed in this context.

# Wikis and blogs

Many social networking tools have now collaborated with each other to offer multiple services and products; as you access the services from one company, it offers blogs, wikis and business networking all in one mixing pot. For example, ZoomInfo (*http://www.zoominfo.com/*) will prompt you to join Zing when you register.

## Wikis

Wikis are web pages that are created with capabilities built in for the purpose of allowing others to amend and update the pages and content. The most obvious example is Wikipedia (*http://www.wikipedia.org/*), which defines a wiki at *http://en.wikipedia.org/wiki/Wiki* (Figure 5.13).

I use Wikipedia occasionally, but I am careful about how I use it, and use it mainly to assist in homework. It is somewhat unnerving knowing that Joe Public can amend the content of another's expertise and those amendments may slip through quality checks. Always double-check the facts you obtain from Wikipedia elsewhere, or assess the author's credentials.

**Figure 5.13** Definition of 'wiki' on Wikipedia

# Blogs

A blog is a weblog and anyone can set up and write one in about five minutes. The software provided for this application is totally intuitive and extremely easy to use, and there are millions of blogs written and updated every day on every topic imaginable. You don't need a website to launch it from, but you can use one if you want to; all the tools are provided by the service organisation and it's free.

I read lots of blogs, mainly on business topics, but also for fun. I've loaded some via RSS feeds onto my desktop. Check out the Shifted Librarian or the Obnoxious Librarian from Hades, or blogs on the demise of Lehman Brothers. Blogs are the writings of people's personal thoughts or their responses to them or to something else, such as a news item. Some blogs are people's rants when they feel very strongly about certain issues, and articulate their frustrations via this medium. Search for them by topic, country, author or other criteria.

Figure 5.14 shows a blog from Vietnam.

After hunting around in Africa for a while, I thought that the World Bank African business blog seemed the most appropriate blog for some serious commentary. Others that I delved through had more social topics (football) and anti-social topics (shooting people) as a high priority for discussion. Some blogs were in more than one language, which is good,

**Figure 5.14**   A blog from Vietnam on Best Blogs

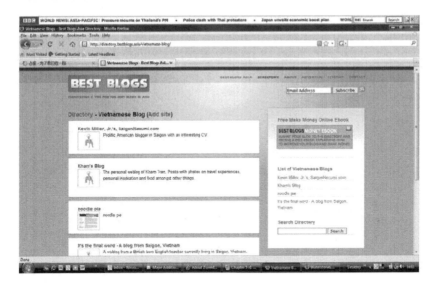

and others provided videos, podcasts and other formats for accessing information.

Figure 5.15 shows an example from the Doing Business Blog (*http://blog .doingbusiness.org/search_results.html?cx=00342607844925513032 8: fvr_ntjnzqi&cof=FORID:11&q=africa&sa=Go*).

**Figure 5.15**   A blog about São Tomé on Doing Business Blog

Ryze: *http://onlinesocialnetworks.blogspot.com/2008/08/
ryze-business-netorking.html*

Ryze is a social networking organisation offering free and fee-based services to many different communities, including the business community (Figures 5.16 and 5.17). It allows members to create blogs.

**Figure 5.16** The Ryze business networking site (1)

**Figure 5.17** The Ryze business networking site (2)

It includes blogs created in the higher education community, where the tutor loads up course work for students, and they interact online with discussions about their work. Many different groups can be located, covering individual professional and business interests.

## Blog software tools

### WordPress.com: *http://wordpress.com*

WordPress.com contains 3,795,025 blogs that you can access, for example the Irresponsible Rumours blog (*http://wordpress.com/tag/ irresponsible-rumours/*). See Figure 5.18.

WordPress.com is just one of many blog software tools that are available on the internet. Blogger is probably the best known. Start your own blog or access the writings of others and add your own commentary.

## The negative impacts of blogs

Not all that is written is of a positive nature, and some blogs can have negative impacts on businesses and people. Some negative communications get posted in the electronic press – especially on blogs related to articles, and even if negative postings are removed within a

**Figure 5.18**    Blog about irresponsible rumours on WordPress.com

short time, if someone spots them, they get sent on. There are further implications related to industrial espionage, which can be publicly displayed if the writer is unaware of the damage that can be caused by what they have written. So there are opportunities here for the disgruntled ex-employee who drops internal corporate information into the public domain to exploit the technology.

## Cybersmearing – corporate rumours – blawgs (legal blogs)

Over the years there have been a number of places to go to hunt out information that companies would not want their competitors to know about. Some of the ones I used have now been shut down, and not least for their names – f**ked companies.com is a prime example – but the information provided was highly controversial and damaging. Companies must constantly monitor what is being written about them, and where this information originates from. Some have internal blogs, which are used to gather feedback from their employees, but with e-mail now a basic communication tool, it doesn't take much for leaks to occur.

An interesting blog exists by the Blogging Journalist (*http://www* *.thebloggingjournalist.com/2006/03/cybersmearing_i.html*), which ponders the difference between defamation and payback by the cybersmearer. There's a fine line between libellous commentary and personal opinion. The Blogging Journalist provides a long list of resources and blogs from this page.

So, if it's not libellous, where does freedom of speech become censorship? What can't be written?

### Reporters Without Borders: *http://www.rsf.org/*

Reporters Without Borders defends journalists who are imprisoned or persecuted for doing their job and fights against censorship that undermines press freedom (Figure 5.19).

Reporters Without Borders publishes a World Press Freedom Index (*http://anonymouse.org/cgi-bin/anon-www.cgi/http://www.rsf.org/article* *.php3?id_article=24025*), which demonstrates the level of censorship inflicted on the media (Figure 5.20).

In 2008 *The Times* reported that civil servants were to be restricted or banned from interaction on blogs and social networking sites after Whitehall and Westminster were embarrassed by blogging disclosures of an employee.[5]

**Figure 5.19** Article about Abdallah Ibn al-Saud on the Reporters Without Borders website

**Figure 5.20** Article about Eritrea on the Reporters Without Borders website

# Virtual worlds

As social networks evolve, they have more sophisticated features built in. A very fast-developing community is the virtual world, and many social networks offer this new concept to their current users. They must keep up with the competition in order to survive, and provide access to the next generation of communication software.

### Second Life: *http://secondlife.com/*

Second Life is a three-dimensional concept, where one can interact online in 'person' in a virtual world in the form of an avatar. A few of the many offerings range from making your avatar, giving it a name, dressing it and adding body decorations. The creation of Linden Research Inc, this virtual world offers a large range of places to visit, chat, shop, listen to music and buy land using Linden dollars. You can travel to many places to 'interact' with other avatars and groups, including those who work in the same industry as you. The Special Libraries Association (SLA) has a presence on Second Life where other information professionals who are SLA members can network, by registering in the first instance and creating an avatar.

I found that learning to use Second Life requires patience, and was not as intuitive as it seemed at first glance, so I took a remote training course in the evenings, courtesy of SLA, to start me off. There's a lot to read in order to learn to use it proficiently. However, it's an interesting way to network, and enjoyable to use. As with all social networking tools, Second Life has non-professional communities, but it is possible to travel to other places to avoid them.

### Kaneva: *http://www.kaneva.com/*

Kaneva is another virtual world. Its website states that 'according to Gartner, over 250 million people will be in virtual worlds by 2011'.

## *The social implications of virtual social networks*

A colleague commented recently that the social implications of these tools could bring a total change in the way that people communicate, and that people may eventually stop going out to meet each other physically. They may sit at home with their computers, interacting with virtual social networks instead. It's a concept that psychologists are

**Figure 5.21**   The home page of Virtual Environments.info

already looking at, for example examining how internet companies make social networking sites exclusive so they are more desirable environments for potential users to join.

There is plenty of reading material available on this subject, including output from Virtual Environments.info, *Psychology Today* and PsychCentral. If this subject is of interest, look out for items covering virtual social climbing and virtual friendships. Virtual Environments.info (*http://www.virtualenvironments.info*) provides a virtual environments comparison chart (Figure 5.21).

There is an abundance of blogs and RSS feeds available from this site covering the virtual world and its surrounding issues.

# RSS feeds

RSS or really simple syndication is a means of bringing information to your desk or laptop, without you having to go and hunt for it. It provides simply formatted information uploaded regularly from a website, with a hyperlink to the full text.

Early on in the development of RSS, you needed an aggregator to pull in RSS feeds to your computer. RSS Compendium produced a huge selection of aggregators, which could be used for this purpose. Browser applications now have these aggregators built in, but you can choose which ones to use, and many web pages and sites offer a good selection. You can also load blogs via RSS and read the updates from the feed.

Today, RSS is a feature on almost every web page accessed, and it takes just seconds to subscribe to these feeds. It is advisable to be quite picky about your RSS selections otherwise you can get swamped by the sheer volume of information arriving on the electronic doorstep.

The RSS Compendium Blog is at *http://rsscompendiumblog.blogspot .com/* (Figure 5.22)

RSS offers the researcher a way to work through large amounts of information, making selections by scanning or speed-reading headlines and the first two sentences of each item. However, some blogs arrive in full text format – like the Silk Road International Blog (*http:// silkroadintl.net/blog/*) (Figure 5.23).

## Copyright of RSS feeds

Users of RSS are bound by the copyright of the website owner, the copyright of the source of the content, and the rights of the author. Therefore if the information accessed is not for personal use, the correct permissions must be sought in advance. If in doubt, source the

**Figure 5.22** The RSS Compendium Blog

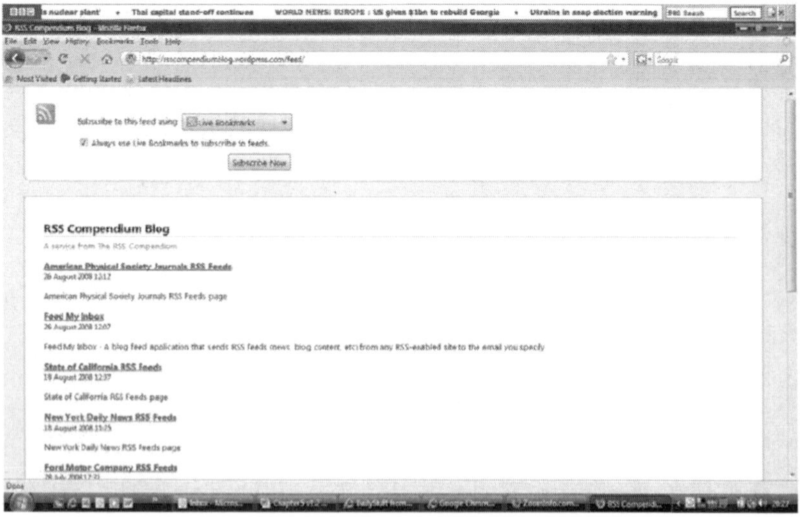

**Figure 5.23** The Silk Road International Blog

information properly, drop the website owner an e-mail, and ask for permission to use their data. If permission to use the information is granted, don't forget to cite the source properly. There are many styles for citation, which can be located on the internet via an educational portal. Use a citation style that is pertinent to your location or legal jurisdiction. Many of these portals also cover the subject of plagiarism.

### HowStuffWorks: *http://feeds.howstuffworks.com/DailyStuff?format=xml*

HowStuffWorks (HSW) is an example of an RSS feed that I pull in daily via a browser. It is a fun but also a useful tool for homework and to find the answers to random questions so often posed by the young. There is a website for HSW in Brazil and China. See Figure 5.24.

Although it provides basic answers to questions and is marketed at a general audience, HSW can be used for business purposes. Answers give enough information for readers to research the subject elsewhere, by picking out relevant keywords. There is a disclaimer on the website on the reliability of the content; the assumption is that content errors can be made, even though the corporate owner of the site is a high quality organisation and reliable.

**Figure 5.24**   Example page of DailyStuff from HowStuffWorks

These are some of the questions HSW has answered:

- How do zombie computers work?
- How does Google work?
- Will the land line phone become obsolete?
- Why does orange juice taste bad after you brush your teeth?
- What are the 10 worst epidemics?
- How do entertainment lawyers work?
- How does NATO work?
- How do recessions work?
- Why is there an underground city beneath Beijing?
- Can the government see what websites I visit?

A daily video is loaded on HSW, which covers topics as diverse as those mentioned above.

# What next?

Social web technology is a growing, thriving network of activity, where the possibilities seem endless and no boundaries will be left uncrossed by the imagination. But as this technology evolves, how will it affect the online population? My mouse in its original form is nearly obsolete, and is now replaced by flat bed mice built into the laptop, along with the web cam and many devices that connect to many other devices.

More and more people live alone now. Are we eventually going to turn into 'virtual' people who stay home alone, and conduct a solitary social and business life via camera, touch screen and voice recognition equipment?

# List of websites mentioned in this chapter

Blogger *https://www.blogger.com/start*
Blogging Journalist *http://www.thebloggingjournalist.com/2006/03/cybers mearing_i.html*
Fortune, 'Bosses behaving badly' *http://money.cnn.com/galleries/2007/fortune/ 0712/gallery.dumbest_bosses.fortune/*
FraudWatch International *http://www.fraudwatchinternational.com*
HowStuffWorks *http://feeds.howstuffworks.com/DailyStuff?format=xml*
Internet World Stats *http://www.internetworldstats.com/stats.htm*
Obnoxious Librarian from Hades *http://olfh.blogspot.com/*
Privacy International *http://www.privacyinternational.org*
PsychCentral *http://psychcentral.com*
Psychology Today *http://psychologytoday.com*
Reporters Without Borders *http://www.rsf.org/*
RSS Compendium Blog *http://rsscompendiumblog.wordpress.com/feed/*
Ryze *http://onlinesocialnetworks.blogspot.com/2008/08/ryze-business-netorking .html*
Second Life *http://secondlife.com/*
Shifted Librarian *http://www.theshiftedlibrarian.com/*
Silk Road International Blog *http://silkroadintl.net/blog/*
Skype™ *http://www.skype.com/intl/en-gb/*
Sophos *http://www.sophos.com*
Wikipedia *http://en.wikipedia.org/*
Women's Institute *http://www.thewi.org.uk/*
WordPress Irresponsible Rumours blog *http://wordpress.com/tag/irresponsible-rumours/*
World Bank African Blog *http://blog.doingbusiness.org/search_results.html? cx=003426078449255130328:fvr_ntjnzqi&cof=FORID:11&q=africa &sa=Go*

YouTube *http://www.youtube.com*
YouTube Google's Chrome browser *http://www.google.com/support/chrome/bin/answer.py?answer=95451&hl=en_GB*
Virtual Environments.info *http://www.virtualenvironments.info/*
ZoomInfo *http://www.zoominfo.com/*

# Notes

1. Privacy International, 'A race to the bottom: privacy ranking of internet service companies', at *http://www.privacyinternational.org/article.shtml?cmd [347]=x-347-553961*
2. See *http://www.fraudwatchinternational.com/phishing/individual_alert.php? fa_no=234791*.
3. Sophos, *Security Threat Report 2008*, at *http://www.sophos.com/sophos/docs/eng/marketing_material/sophos-security-report-08.pdf*.
4. 'Spam shame continues for USA as UK exits dirty dozen, Sophos reports', 28 April 2009, at *http://www.sophos.com/pressoffice/news/articles/2009/04/dirtydozen.html*.
5. Jill Sherman, 'Civil Service bloggers facing tough new rules', *The Times*, 11 March 2008, p. 8.

# 6

# Conclusion

Now you know the world really is at your fingertips. I believe that lateral thinking is one of the main ways to find information, and by using different tools one can access what one really needs using less complex syntax. Competent research skills are there to see and interact with when you know how. You can sit in a virtual world and 'sunbathe' but it isn't real. You can talk to a colleague or business partner thousands of miles away, and see them and it is real. You can also have a connection when you are a conference speaker with another person on the other side of the world, or teach an injured child remotely. You can check out your next prospective employee.

Those who lack basic transport or communications infrastructures are the poorest people who don't have access to these services, but as they become cheaper it is getting easier for the poorest to access the services via their mobile phones or educational institutions.

The online world is a serious place to be, whether you are placing an online shopping delivery order or networking with like-minded individuals who share a great interest in the same industry as you, or talking on instant messaging to people who are mentally hurt in their world. The world is small now, but it can be abused if some feel the need to do that.

This hub of human interactivity from remote places is a phenomenon that I have been lucky to be part of. I have had professional relationships with people I've not met yet, and with others who I have. My biggest and happiest experience was meeting Indian colleagues from the Special Libraries Association in New Delhi last year. It's a great position to be in. Walk the trail and discover it for yourself. We talk electronically and then one day we meet face to face.

By the time my sons are old enough to read this book, they may say 'Mum – this is really old fashioned!' And I would say, 'Not in my time it wasn't.' I won't give them all the tricks of the trade right now as they are too young to use them, but I have a couple of Google books that they might like to start honing their skills with when they are ready.

It has been a pleasure to write this book and I hope you enjoyed it and learn something from the content.

# 7

# Fun stuff

And finally... Some stuff for fun, learning, the bizarre, or just because it's out there for the taking. I read the sites listed below because I enjoy reading them. I don't make judgements on the writings of others. They express their thoughts and opinions, and the diversity is stimulating. I hope you enjoyed this book and can put some of it to good use. I change my reading materials all the time, and find writers who hit the spot for me. Blogging is easy and fun, as you know.

So here is a small selection of my current list of favourites:

- Aardvark – Resources for Librarians *http://www.aardvarknet.info/ user/aardvarkwelcome/* Asian and Pacific-centric, but loaded with good information, news, journals, conferences, tech, articles and more.

- Conan the Librarian *http://weblogs.elearning.ubc.ca/physio/2006/12/ conan_the_librarian.php* Speaks for itself.

- Freepint *http://www.freepint.com/* A must-have for serious information professionals. I have contributed to this site because I like the relevant, highly professional content.

- Harvard Business School Working Knowledge *http://hbswk.hbs.edu/* Specific gems available, although faculty-related. Subscribe to the weekly newsletter and be selective.

- Internet Evolution *http://www.internetevolution.com/default.asp?f_ src=ieupdate* Commentary and products on the future of the internet.

- Librarian in Black *http://librarianinblack.typepad.com/*

- Librarians do it quietly *http://kimle1311.wordpress.com/* Old – but good.

- Lifehacker *http://lifehacker.com/* Learn more about hardware and software. A good website!

- March of the Librarians *http://www.youtube.com/watch?v= Td922l0NoDQ* Another oldie, but a look at the 2007 American Library Association conference from another (outsider?) perspective.

- North Korean Economy Watch *http://www.nkeconwatch.com/2009/ 02/07/the-russian-market-for-used-lightbulbs/* A diverse range of subjects.

- Obnoxious Librarian from Hades Blog *http://olfh.blogspot.com/* A blog from a librarian working for the fictitional 'Hades Corporation', who lives in another musical generation (rock music from the 1960s and 70s) with a diverse sense of humour.

- Paul Kedrosky's Infectious Greed *http://paul.kedrosky.com/archives/ 2009/02/06/the_chart_that.html* As someone with an investment banking background, I really enjoy this. He is also a Nouriel Roubini fan (RGE Monitor).

- Pew Research Centre *http://pewresearch.org/* Just because its US-centric, don't ignore this. It's good for statistics and a good starting place for building a bigger picture.

- Phil Bradley *http://www.philb.com/* Internet guru. Blog, country engines, presentations, articles, fun and more. A lively speaker who knows his stuff.

- Quirk's Marketing Research Review *http://www.quirks.com/* Loads of information before you even buy a report.

- Rejecting the Stereotypical Librarian Image *http://warriorlibrarian .com/IMHO/stereo.html*.

- Search Engine College *http://www.searchenginecollege.com/free-newsletter.shtml* Free, interesting newsletter and they respond to tech questions.

- Shorelines Newsletter *http://shore.com/commentary/newsletter/* Good non-judgemental information.

- Stephen Arnold's Blog: Beyond Search *http://arnoldit.com/wordpress/* As far as search engine tech is concerned, Stephen Arnold takes no prisoners. Critical analysis for the big search engine players, and when he finds good stuff, he talks about it. A great writer and speaker. I've seen him speak at three conferences (so far...).

- The Darwin Awards *http://www.darwinawards.com/* Described as 'a chronicle of enterprising demises honoring [sic] those who improve the species... by accidentally removing themselves from it'. This is a website dedicated to the most bizarre ways that people have managed to die or very badly hurt themselves. If you have a slightly warped sense of humour, this is one for you!

- The Open Directory's Librariana: Humour *http://www.dmoz.org/ Reference/Libraries/Library_and_Information_Science/Librariana/Humor/* Take your pick.

- Warrior Librarian's Original Library Humour *http://warriorlibrarian .com/deweyindex.html* In Dewey shelf order – of course!

If you want more, read the blog! *http://globalresearcher.wordpress.com/.*

# Index